THE PROSPEROUS AUTHOR: HOW TO MAKE A LIVING WITH YOUR WRITING

DEVELOPING A MILLIONAIRE MINDSET

CASSANDRA GAISFORD

THE PROSPEROUS AUTHOR:
HOW TO MAKE A LIVING WITH YOUR WRITING

Book One: Developing A Millionaire Mindset

Cassandra Gaisford, BCA, Dip Psych

PRAISE FOR THE PROSPEROUS AUTHOR

"What I really like about *The Prosperous Author* is that it is a great book to read before you even put pen to paper. There are a zillion books on the market which tell us how to market and publish our books. This book stands apart from the rest in that it gets your head in the right mindset to create the best possible book.

The Prosperous Author is overflowing with wonderful, motivating and thought-provoking quotes from bestselling and award-winning authors as samples and inspiration. This may be Cassandra's finest book yet."

~ Mimi Emmanuel, author of *The Holy Grail of Book Publishing*

"Cassandra Gaisford has molded a helpful resource in her latest publication *The Prosperous Author*. Together with helpful ideas encouraging readers to believe in their writing, or in my case in my project, she also presents challenges to motivate the reader, well-chosen examples of successful writers, and honest offerings of her own journey.

This book provides well-researched ideas to support anyone who has a dream to believe in themselves and go for gold and develop that dream into reality. It is not just for writers, it is for all of us who have a golden nugget of a dream and want to bring it to full creation."

~ Catherine Sloan, counsellor

"A lot of great insights on how to become a more positive, passionate and prosperous writer. I loved the second part of the book, 'Cultivate a Burning Desire.' It really motivates me and inspires me to see how successful writers think and act. I like the resources and ideas Cassandra Gaisford gave throughout. There were also some great quotes that I liked a lot. I'll definitely refer back to this book in the future to assist me on my personal journey to become a prosperous writer!"

~ Thibaut Meurisse, blogger

"Author Cassandra Gaisford has brought a much needed book to the self-publishing market. The author of the popular *Mid-Life Career Rescue* series has published multiple books on Amazon and is now sharing her secrets as a successful author in this latest book, *The Prosperous Author: How to Make a Living With Your Writing*.

The Prosperous Author is a great read that really dives into the mindset of what it means to not just prosper financially but to live a successful and well-balanced life based on health, happiness and close relationships. This book is definitely for the reader who lacks self-esteem and wants more of it, wants to overcome perfectionism, or has doubt and uncertainty and needs to break beyond these barriers. *The Prosperous Author* can show you how to do all of that.

This book really has a positive impact on one's mindset. As the author points out in her key message throughout the book, mindset is at the core of all our success. It creates emotion and motivation. It brings us up or keeps us down.

The book wastes no time and jumps right into 'the millionaire mindset.' We can learn how to think like a millionaire and how to develop the strategies and apply them to our life for attracting more influence and money. By programming your subconscious beliefs, you are rewiring your own brain for success. The author teaches us to nurture our thoughts and cast out the negative seeds that are growing there. We can see that attitude is everything.

Energy is another great topic discussed. We can boost our energy by cutting away the relationships and negative influences holding us back. This is one of my favorite chapters in the book. We can 'relive our life story' too, by imagining the life that we could have instead of the life that we wished we had had. Then, in the chapter 'Blossom,' we learn to pay attention to divine creativity, intuition, and signs of manifestation.

Cassandra gets into the topic of passion and we can see how cultivating a passionate lifestyle frees us up to pursue life's gifts; and to craft our writing into a solid piece of reading material. Write with your purpose and the words will flow much easier.

This book really hits home for me as an author *and* someone who is dedicated to carving out purpose, passion and a life of more wealth and health. Every chapter ends with a positive wrap-up ['Mining for Gold'] of the important lessons learned.

The other great chapters will teach you how to:

Dream big, create a new destiny and turn a profit as a successful author. My favorite chapters here are:

Keeping deadlines. Without deadlines, how can we get our work finished? There are solid strategies here for doing just that. As Cassandra points out as well, we can become prosperous authors by journaling our way to success, staying focused on the task, keeping doubt out, sticking with perseverance, and believing in yourself to get the job done.

This book is well-written, structured and serves as an excellent resource for authors and people looking to fill up their lives with positivity for achieving their goals and objectives.

A definite 'Good Read' recommendation."

~ Scott Allan, author of *Do It Scared*

*For Lorenzo
whose mantra
"Show me the money!"
inspires me to succeed.*

EPILOGUE

There Will Come a Moment ...
When your life begins to unfold with new and wonderful events, there will come a moment that you will be in awe, wonder, and utter wakefulness when you realize it was your mind that created them. In your rapture, you will look back from this vantage point at your entire life, and you will not want to change anything. You will not regret any action or feel bad about whatever has happened to you, because in that moment of your manifestation, it will all make sense to you. You will see how your past got you to this great state.

~ Dr. Joe Dispenza, author

AUTHOR'S NOTE

I've been a published non-fiction writer for over ten years, penning articles for newspapers and magazines. Most of the time I wrote for free. My motivation? I wanted to provide helpful tips and strategies for people who couldn't afford my coaching and psychology fees.

I also started writing inspirational workbooks for career and life coaching clients who were sent to me for help by their workplaces—but only given two or three paid hours of support. Early on, before Kindle became the phenomenon that it is now, I began thinking of ways I could help more people with my words of self-help and empowerment.

The editor of *Marie Claire* Magazine suggested I write a book. The first book I wrote, *Happy at Work for Mid-Lifers,* was turned down by so many publishing houses that I began to get discouraged. They told me, "New Zealander's aren't ready for passion. It won't sell." I knew they were wrong. So, I decided to back myself and start my own self-publishing company and self-publish. I've since written and released numerous non-fiction books and branched into fiction too—writing romance novels under my pen name Mollie Mathews.

I have self-published over 20 titles in the last two years alone—all them have been #1 bestsellers on Amazon. I have created multiple streams of income—many of them from my writing. Others from my work as a holistic psychologist and coach and also from certifying people to become Worklife Solutions life and career coaches.

People write to me and tell me that are awed by my prosperous productivity and success. But I feel it's so important to let you know that I wasn't always the confident, prosperous author I am today.

For many years I struggled to complete the books I wanted to write. I wrestled unsuccessfully with doubt and fear and other blocks to living a prosperous writing life.

Because of my own limiting beliefs about my writing and my ability to make money as a writer, it took me until my sixteenth book to call myself an author. Even then I struggled. I hadn't gone to University and received an English degree, I didn't train as a journalist. Everything I learned was self-taught.

Happily, I'm a compulsive note-taker and researcher—my partner once said that I'm an obsessive collector of positivity. My goal has always been to overcome obstacles and live my best life—and to help other people achieve the same.

Whenever I'm in a slump or needing an inspirational boost, I turn to people who are smarter or more skilled than me for good advice. Very often, I write a book to self-help my way to prosperity.

If you've been procrastinating, experiencing self-doubt, feeling fearful, or just getting in your own way, you're in good company. I've been there, too—as have many successful people. Guess what, getting in your own way is normal!

I promise there are solutions to the problems you're currently facing—and you'll find them in the pages that follow.

Much of the wisdom contained in this book, the first in The Prosperity for Authors series, derives from the success strategies I've distilled and applied in the last few years—having finally "knocked the buggers off" (to paraphrase one of the first people to climb the summit of Mount Everest, and fellow New Zealander, Sir Edmund Hillary).

Author's Note

As I've already said, after years of starting books and never finishing them, in the past two years I've written, finished, and published twenty bestselling books.

What changed?

My mindset—amongst other things.

In The Prosperity for Authors series, I'll share with you the things I've learned figuring out how to make a living from my writing.

You'll benefit from dozens of insights based on survey research and my professional achievements as a holistic psychologist, bestselling author, and creativity expert.

You'll gain insight into the success secrets of extraordinary authors and creative entrepreneurs from a variety of fiction and non-fiction genres. Tim Ferriss, James Patterson, Paulo Coelho, Nora Roberts, Arianna Huffington, Oprah, and Isabel Allende are just a few of the many creative mentors you'll learn from.

As you'll discover, being prosperous is not just about money; it's also about health, happiness, close relationships, living a meaningful life, and enjoying life's journey.

- If you'd love to find a way to create a living from your writing
- If you suffer from self-doubt or fear of failure
- If you need approval from others
- If you lack confidence or self-esteem
- If you're a perfectionist or find the challenges of a creative life overwhelming
- Or, if you've already embarked on the writer's journey and want to elevate your success

... then *The Prosperous Author: Developing A Millionaire Mindset* is exactly the right book for you. It will show you that these challenges, obstacles, and desires are a critical part of your success.

If you'd like to make a living from your writing, developing a prosperous mindset is the foundation skill from which all else follows.

The ideas described in this book apply to anyone who's trying to inject some prosperous creativity into their life and work.

In short, this book is for you—whoever you are, whatever you ache to create, and however you define prosperity.

INTRODUCTION

...Mindset. There's no getting away from it: that's a crucial part of the puzzle.

~ Mark Dawson, author

"Real artists don't starve," writes Jeff Goins in his latest book titled by the same name.

It's a confronting statement—in part because it's true. Some of the most successful authors today are making serious coin from their writing.

Former welfare beneficiary J.K. Rowling is a millionaire many times over. James Patterson, the son of an insurance salesman, earns so much he was able to donate over $26 million US dollars to institutions supporting higher learning.

But Goins' assertion is confronting because it's also untrue.

Historical archives are littered with the failure stories of talented, prolific, memorable writers and artists who never experienced financial success in their lifetimes.

Vincent Van Gogh never earned a sustainable living and was often destitute.

F. Scott Fitzgerald, once one of the highest paid authors of his generation, died an impoverished, discouraged alcoholic.

As Goins notes in *Real Artists Don't Starve*, "At the time of Fitzgerald's death, *The Great Gatsby* was practically out of print and nowhere to be found in bookstores. His last royalty check was for thirteen dollars, most of which was from copies the author had purchased himself. A once-promising novelist ended his career doing what he considered hack work and went to the grave thinking himself a failure."

Poet and novelist Edgar Allan Poe, credited by many as being the inventor of the detective fiction genre, died penniless.

Oscar Wilde, the flamboyant writer, poet and playwright, was forced into bankruptcy.

And then there are the vast numbers of aspiring authors you'll never hear of who have suffered financially pursuing their dream of making a living from their writing.

Nearly everyone wants to be rich. So, why do only a few reach those heights? How do millions of writers work their fingers to the bone yet end up broke?

. . . and others don't?

It's not about luck.

Many millionaire authors will tell you that luck played a large part in their success. They hit the right idea at the right time in the right place—and you could stop there, assuming that unless you get lucky, you won't get rich.

But then if you look a little deeper, you'll uncover something else, something all prosperous people have in common—the millionaire mindset.

And even more interestingly, millionaires don't have much else in common—there's no standard for academic achievement; there's no commonality of family background; there's no "special knowledge" that these people possess.

It's about your mindset.

When it comes down to it, success flows from the habits, attitudes and behaviors you use *every day* that move you, step-by-step, towards millionaire status.

And yes, sometimes even the rich go belly up, but something they never lose is their millionaire mindset.

What is a millionaire mindset?

- Millionaires think big; they may start off with small goals, but they always have a big goal in mind
- Millionaires aren't afraid to fail. They play to win, not to avoid defeat
- Millionaires focus on what they want—and go for it
- Millionaires are goal-orientated
- Millionaires focus on growth; they know comfort stunts progress
- Millionaires look to monetize everything
- Millionaires accumulate money; sometimes they appear stingy, but they know being frugal is the way to grow their bank balance
- Millionaires never stop learning; they pursue greatness and they invest in continual improvement
- Millionaires learn from their mistakes
- Millionaires maintain a positive mindset
- Millionaires know that success attracts success; they learn from and surround themselves with only the best
- Millionaires enjoy attention—if not on themselves personally, then on their brand. They're tireless self-promoters and know that attention attracts money

By thinking like a millionaire and applying the success secrets of highly successful authors, you'll maximise your likelihood of success.

Your goal may not be to make millions—your goal may be to enjoy following your passion for telling stories and to have fun doing it.

You may wish to earn a small living from your writing—or a grand one. You may wish to prepare your mindset for the day you decide to tackle your writing project.

Whatever your intention, in this book you'll learn how to develop a winning mindset so that you thrive, not just survive, as an author.

Although this book was written for writers, the principles and strategies can be embraced by business entrepreneurs, actors, dancers, painters, photographers, filmmakers, and thousands of others around the world who want to enhance their mindsets.

Your 5-Step Blueprint To True Success

It takes a certain amount of discipline. I guarantee you that it is the discipline that will pay off.

~ James Patterson, author

Developing a prosperous mindset is the foundation skill from which all else follows.

The first book in The Prosperity for Authors series, *How to Make a Living from your Writing: Developing a Millionaire Mindset*, takes a holistic look at what it means, and what it takes to develop, a prosperous mindset.

Through inspiring anecdotes of successful creatives both past and present, and by following the 5-Step Blueprint to True Success, you'll discover that making a living from your writing is not only doable, it's also a fulfilling way to live an extraordinary life.

The Five Principles of Prosperity

I've sectioned *Developing a Millionaire Mindset* into clusters of principles. Principles aren't constricting rules incapable of being shaped, but rather general and fundamental truths which may be used to help guide your choices.

Let's look briefly at the five principles of prosperity and what each will cover:

The only way to change your 'outer' world is to first change your 'inner' world. The first step in developing a prosperous mindset is learning how to master the inner game of wealth.

Principle One will teach you how to train your brain to think like a millionaire and program your mind for success.

You'll also discover why a holistic approach to creating a successful writing career is an important part of achieving prosperity.

Principle Two will show you how to intensify your desire, harness the power of passion and purpose, and dream big to elevate your success.

Principle Three will help you shift gears by thinking and acting like a pro. Professionals love numbers, plan for success, finish what they start, and work smart.

Your health is the cornerstone of your wealth, yet it's an area many creatives devalue—until they get a wake-up call. Start smart and invest in healthy routines—you'll learn how in **Principle Four**.

Principle Five will begin the process of slaying any obstacles to success, including unhelpful beliefs, doubt, and sabotaging subconscious scripts that keep you stuck.

In this book you'll learn:

- The secrets to developing a prosperous mindset
- How to define prosperity on your own terms
- How to master the psychology of creation
- How to unlock your potential
- How to overcome the fears that stop you from reaching your fullest potential
- How to fight through your blocks and win your inner creative battles
- How to set and achieve audacious goals
- How to steal from your heroes (rather than waiting for inspiration)

- How to take strategic risks (rather than reckless ones)
- How to overcome your fear of failure, criticism, and change
- How to whip anxiety, despondency and depression into shape
- How to overcome inertia, writer's block, and the resistance of a blank page
- How to identify real priorities that are central to your life and to define work's true meaning
- How to turn pro, tap your inner power, and create your life's work

But mostly what I hope you will gain from this book is encouragement, inspiration, and stimulation if you are, or ever hope to be, a writer.

How To Use This Book

Think of *The Prosperous Author* like a shot of espresso. Sometimes one quick hit is all it takes to get started. But sometimes you need a few shots to sustain your energy. Or maybe you need a bigger motivational hit and then you're on your way.

You're in control of what works best for you. Go at your own pace, but resist over-caffeinating. A little bit of guidance here and there can do as much to fast-track your success as consuming all the principles in one hit.

Skim to sections that are most relevant to you, and return to familiar ground to reinforce home-truths. But most of all, enjoy your experience.

Mining for Gold

Apply the principles which follow by journaling your responses to the questions and challenges presented at the end of each chapter.

"I love your works to date—provocative and supportive at the same time," a gentleman who'd read my *Mid-Life Career Rescue* books wrote to me.

To provoke is to incite or stimulate. It's the reason I've included open-ended questions and calls to action in each guide. The best questions are open, generative ones that don't allow for "yes/no" answers; rather, they encourage you to tap into your higher wisdom and intuition, or to go in search of answers—as successful people do.

"I really like the questions at the end of each chapter—'Mining for Gold.' They challenge my thinking; they provide me with opportunities to move forward with my own project; and overall they bring a well-rounded focus to what has been written in the preceding section/chapter," a reader of this book wrote to me.

Dive Deeper with *The Prosperous Author Workbook*

The Prosperous Author will also be available as a printed workbook, with space to write your responses to the challenges and calls to action within the book.

Expand Your Learning—Follow My Blog

Dive deeper into some of the insights I've shared and sign up for my newsletter at http://eepurl.com/cQXY4f and follow my blog—navigate to www.cassandragaisford.com.

Re-read My Other Books

"Re-reading books has been one of my secrets to success, because more often than not, I miss some (or most) of the good stuff the first time around," says Bryan Cohen, author and co-creator of the "Sell More Books Show" (sellmorebooksshow.com).

Cohen continues, "Even if I caught the goodies on read number one, it's very possible I didn't *apply* the information to my career or actually *complete* the exercises within."

Have you ever been guilty of skipping over the exercises in a book or failing to experiment and try some of its tips and strategy methods? I know I have.

That's why I think you should re-read not just my books, but any others you found inspiring.

Visit my author's page and remind yourself of the books you've already read—or would love to read.

Inspirational Quotes to Support and Empower

Sometimes all it takes is one encouraging word, one timely bit of advice to awaken your power within. Throughout *The Prosperous Author* I've added a variety of short sound-bites of wisdom—choosing from a wide range of super-capable men and women, historical and current, young and old.

They are men and women who share your dreams and had to overcome significant obstacles on the way to prosperity and success.

Be Empowered

Empowerment is defined as giving power or authority to someone or something—who better to decide who assumes this power and sovereign authority than you.

Empowered people do what they need to do to assume mastery over their thoughts, feelings, emotions, and things that affect their lives.

Empowered people are successful people because they live life on their own terms; they do the things that really matter to them and those they love.

Empowered people are resilient in the face of setbacks, disappointments, or attacks, and they're flexible enough to tackle obstacles in their paths.

They recognise that they are the experts and sovereign authority in their lives. They learn from, and surround themselves with, other empowered, successful people. They back themselves even when they don't succeed.

Are you ready to heed the call for prosperity?

Let's get going...

YOUR MILLIONAIRE MIND

1

WHAT IS PROSPERITY?

The privilege of a lifetime is being who you are.

~ Joseph Campbell, author

Prosperity is hard to define, but easy to see and feel when achieved. Being prosperous isn't necessarily about how much money you have, how many homes you own, or any of the other things people obsessed with material possessions covet.

Dictionary.com defines prosperity as, "a successful, flourishing, or thriving condition, especially in financial respects." Other definitions of prosperity include, "the condition of prospering; success or wealth."

The history of the word prosperity stems from the 12th century Old French word *prosprete*—derived from the Latin word *prosperitatem* which translates to "good fortune."

For increasing numbers of people, good fortune or being prosperous includes: living authentically; maintaining good health; and having fulfilling relationships, creative freedom, a sense of well-being, peace of mind, happiness and joy.

Prosperity, for some people, means achieving financial freedom. Prosperity also includes the ability to achieve your desires, whatever these may be, and being true to the vision you have for yourself and your life.

Coco Chanel once said, "There are people who have money and people who are rich. How many cares one loses when one decides not to be something, but to be someone."

When you commit to being the creator of your life and defining prosperity on your own terms, you choose to enrich your life and you become "*someone.*" If earning a living from your writing is your goal, you choose to become a successful author.

Mining for Gold

What does prosperity mean to you? Would a passive income that funds your lifestyle fit the bill? What about living and working anywhere in the world? Or do you need truckloads of sales on Amazon and buckets of savings in the bank to classify your life as "prosperous?"

How will you know when you have succeeded? Who are you, or who will you become?

What will the first line be in the story of your prosperous life?

2
WHAT DO YOU BELIEVE?

A large income is the best recipe for happiness I have heard of.

~ Jane Austen

"Research shows that 80 percent of individuals will never be financially free in the way they'd like to be, and 80 percent will never claim to be truly happy," writes T. Harv Eker in his book *Secrets of the Millionaire Mind: Mastering the Inner Game of Wealth*.

"The reason is simple," Eker writes, "Most people are unconscious. They are a little asleep at the wheel. They work and think on a superficial level of life—based only on what they can see. They live strictly in the visible world."

Yet, many of the things that influence your thoughts, feelings, and behaviours are invisible; a great many lurk in the realm of the subconscious mind.

The function of your subconscious mind is to store and retrieve data. Its job is to ensure that you respond exactly the way you are programmed.

"By the time you reach the age of 21, you've already permanently stored more than one hundred times the contents of the entire Encyclopaedia Britannica," says motivational writer Brian Tracey.

And much of this information is rubbish, false, incomplete, or obsolete.

REPROGRAMMING Your Subconscious Beliefs

Your subconscious mind is like a huge memory bank. Its capacity is virtually unlimited. It permanently stores everything that ever happens to you. What is limited is your ability to consciously recall many of the scripts programmed into your mind.

You may not even be aware of limiting beliefs that are holding you back or placing a cap on your ability to earn a living from your writing.

One of the most important things you can commit to realising is that you exist in more than the physical world. The mental world, the emotional world, and the spiritual world all exert a powerful influence over you—whether you are consciously tapping into them or not.

"What most people never realise is that the physical realm is merely a 'printout' of the other three," writes T. Harv Eker.

Any limiting and unhelpful beliefs or repressed experiences preventing you from becoming a prosperous author cannot be changed in the physical world. They can only be changed in the "program"—the mental, emotional, and spiritual worlds.

Which is why *The Prosperous Author: Developing a Millionaire Mindset* takes a holistic approach to success. Passion, joy, faith, prayer, dreams, purpose, and mindfulness practices are some of the strategies we'll discuss in this book.

You'll also learn how to develop a rock-solid belief in your ability to succeed. Building firm self-confidence will help you beat the naysayers and weather the inevitable setbacks with ease.

. . .

MINING FOR GOLD

How can you harness the power of the mental, emotional and spiritual worlds to reprogram your beliefs?

What evidence-based explanations do you have for the beliefs or rules you follow? How might the opposite also be true? How can you adjust your thinking?

3

YOUR MONEY BLUEPRINT

It's not enough to be in the right place at the right time. You have to be the right person in the right place at the right time.

~ T. Harv Eker

Your financial blueprint consists of a combination of your thoughts, feelings, and actions related to money.

It's formed primarily during childhood and the information or "programming" you received in the past. Imprinted upon you by parents, siblings, friends, authority figures, teachers, religious leaders, media, your culture, and other influential sources later in life, your beliefs, you sometimes find, are mistaken.

You may have heard, as I did growing up, that you'll never make a living from art. Or that art doesn't contribute anything of value to society.

The chances are high that you were actively discouraged and channeled into supposedly more "prosperous" or socially sanctioned pursuits, like being a lawyer or a doctor—or a good wife!

As Jeff Goins notes, for years, the fallacy of the starving artist has pervaded our culture, leaching into the minds of creative people and stifling their dreams.

But the evidence-based truth is that the world's most successful authors and artists do not starve. They thrive by leveraging off the power of their millionaire mindset and by capitalising on their creative strengths.

Your thoughts and what you believe to be true for you influences your feelings, your energy, and ultimately your behaviour.

What you believe, consciously or unconsciously, sets your income threshold.

Prosperous authors are never content with just scraping by. They believe they have the potential to create unlimited wealth—and they set out to achieve it.

So who are you? How do you think? What are your beliefs? What are your habits and traits? How do you really feel about money and your earning potential?

Answering these initial questions, and those below, will help your journey toward prosperity. You'll learn more strategies to help boost your self-awareness and co-create new liberating beliefs throughout this book.

Mining for Gold

What unhelpful beliefs were programmed into you as a child?

What messages have you heard, or do you continue to hear, about making a living from your art?

How are these messages influencing you?

Do you believe it's possible to make a substantial living from your writing? On a scale of 1-10, 10 being highest, what is the level of your self-belief?

4

CULTIVATE A SUCCESS MINDSET

*You cannot help being good,
because your hand and your mind,
being accustomed to gather flowers
would ill know how to pluck thorns.*

~ Leonardo da Vinci

His Holiness the 14th Dalai Lama once said, "Negative thoughts are like weeds, but positive thoughts are like flowers—they need nurturing every day."

Leonardo da Vinci proactively fertilised his mind and empowered his resolve by focusing on his dreams, goals, and aspirations.

To steady himself against self-doubt or the attacks of others, he actively cultivated a success mindset by using affirmations, journaling, meditating, channeling and accessing the spiritual realms, and surrounding himself with like-minded, aspirational and inspirational people. By doing so, he developed grit.

If you actively cultivate a success mindset you automatically increase your prosperity because your mind, focused on the fruits of your positive intention and effort, will create a barrier to discouragement. This keeps away the thorns of self-doubt, procrastination, fear, and any of the other things toxic to your success.

Oprah once said that one of the best ways to cultivate a success mindset is to think like a queen: "A queen is not afraid to fail. Failure is another stepping stone to greatness."

Similarly, J.K. Rowling encourages making failure part of your success strategy. "Failure is inevitable—make it a strength," she says.

Mining for Gold

Sometimes your greatest weakness is your greatest strength. If fear of failure is holding you back, identify ways to make it part of your success mindset.

Attitude is everything. How can you think like a king or queen and cultivate a success mindset?

5

ELEVATE YOUR ENERGY

The key to success is to raise your own energy; when you do, people will naturally be attracted to you. And when they show up, bill 'em!

~ Stuart Wilde, author

Everything is energy, and energy is everything. Without it you have nothing. But you don't want sad, bad, defeatist energy—that won't help at all.

Passion, joy, and love are the highest vibrations you can feel. They're the rocket-fuel feelings that will catapult you to success.

"The two most inspiring life forces are anger and joy," singer-songwriter Alanis Morissette once said, "I could write 6 zillion songs about these two feelings alone."

As you'll discover in my earlier book, *Find Your Passion and Purpose: Four Easy Steps to Discover a Job You Want and Live the Life You Love*, and later in this book, anger can be a constructive force for positive change. But the more moments you spend being happy and joyful, and allowing yourself and your work to be infused with this positive energy, the closer you are to being the God force of all life. You evoke the power of the laws of attraction and abundance, and you attract prosperity.

"If you will live your life in such a manner—that everything you pursue is to make yourself happy—you will live your life to its grandest destiny," writes Ramtha in *The White Book*.

"Joy begets joy, for when you accept the joy that is pressed to you, that joy heightens the joy of your tomorrows and opens you up for ever greater receivership."

Co-creating with joy, passion, Spirit, and love and creating and maintaining a positive mindset are essential ingredients in raising your energy.

Don't worry if you don't know what makes you happy or feel joyful or you haven't figured out where your passions lie. You'll dive deeper into this treasure trove of riches as you progress through this book.

What matters now is that you begin with the end in mind and make a commitment to only invest in things that make you feel good and create positive vibrations.

This may require doing some inner work, increasing your self-awareness, and committing to further personal development. It may mean regularly checking in and monitoring your calibration, or it may involve some tough action.

Many successful authors choose to walk away from soul-sucking jobs and relationships to elevate their energy. Paulo Coelho, Isabel Allende, J.K Rowling, Nora Roberts, James Patterson, and Jessie Burton, for example, may not have read Ramtha's sage words which I have quoted below, but they found success by pursuing the love, joy, and passion they discovered when writing.

Importantly, in the process of following their bliss, they all rekindled a deep love for themselves.

"There is no greater purpose in life than to live for the love and fulfilment of self, and that can only be achieved by participating in this life and doing those things which bring you happiness regardless of what they are, for who shall say it is wrong or that it is not good for you?" writes Ramtha in *The White Book*.

Mining for Gold

What daily practices, routines, or habits fill you with joy? Notice the times you feel marvellous.

What soul-sucking jobs, relationships, or situations depress your energy?

How can you manifest feel-good vibrations? Develop a plan to restore positivity to your daily diet.

6

BOOST YOUR SELF-AWARENESS

I had no idea that being your authentic self could make me as rich as I've become. If I had, I'd have done it a lot earlier.

~ Oprah Winfrey

Many of us go through life thinking we are an open book. Yet we are far more multi-faceted and complex than that. What you portray to the world, choose to reveal, or know about yourself are like clouds crossing the sky—ever changing and full of hidden depth.

How can you boost your self-belief and create authentically if you don't know who you are and who you want to be?

"The key to growth is the introduction of higher dimensions of consciousness into our awareness," the philosopher Lao Tzu once wrote.

Many experts believe that you are unable to truly realise your strengths without the objective insight provided by other people. That's why surrounding yourself with people who value and support you, and keeping a praise book or feedback journal, is so important.

Through other people's eyes it becomes possible to confirm strengths you may be aware of but have not truly valued, or to discover gifts that you may have overlooked or discounted.

The power of collecting feedback is powerfully summed up by businesswoman Barbara Koziarski in Kay Douglas' book *Living Out Loud*:

> "I realised that I had been collecting evidence of failures, telling myself 'I can't do this because . . .,' and sometimes they were old failure messages from the past. To overcome my doubts and fears, I started to look for and collect evidence of my success.
>
> "Sometimes people would come up to me and say, 'You really spoke to me. That touched me,' and I'd go home and write that down. So, I started to think that I was worthwhile because I had proof of it. And once I could shore myself up with the external proof I got better at not needing it."

Collecting affirming feedback, personality tests, and even astrological profiles are just some of many helpful tools designed to boost self-awareness. But very often they provide just a small part of the puzzle of discovering your authentic self.

Paying greater attention to the things that stir your soul, ignite your passion, and awaken your heart are also great ways to boost your self-awareness; s is a commitment to experimentation.

As Austin Kleon writes in his excellent book, *Steal Like an Artist*, "If I'd waited to know who I was or what I was about before I started 'being creative,' well, I'd still be sitting around trying to figure myself out instead of making things."

I know from experience that in order to be, you must first do. To be a writer—write. Try different genres and styles and experiment until you find the thing that makes your soul sing.

Neuropsychologist Katherine Benziger says, "People are happiest, healthiest, and most effective when developing, using, and being rewarded for their natural gifts."

. . .

MINING FOR GOLD

Make boosting your awareness of your true essence a priority.

Keep a passion journal and note all the times, people, and events that make your spirit soar. Notice what sparks joy, purpose, or passion. These may provide clues to your gifts and provide subjects you may write successfully about later.

What comes naturally to you? Who are you and what can you do without really trying? What are your superpowers?

List some other ways you could increase your level of self-awareness and decrease your blind spots. You may find it helpful to think about situations in the past where people valued you more than you valued yourself. How did you learn about yourself and all that you were capable of?

How can you do and be what you are?

7
CREATE A NEW LIFE STORY

A girl should be two things: who and what she wants.

~ Coco Chanel

No one will ever know the real Coco Chanel because she designed it that way. She once said, "People's lives are an enigma."

She perpetuated her own mystery by constantly creating a new life story, reinventing her past and weaving threads of fantasy around her family history.

Coco was not proud of her true history. She felt the stigma of her illegitimate birth in a poorhouse to parents who, in the eye of general society, were wandering gypsies.

Coco dreamed of living like a millionaire. It was fantasy that sustained her as a young girl locked in a convent; she imagined a new life—and with it a new story about her background.

She obscured her past from others, refashioning its heartaches and betrayals, smoothing away the rough edges. She reengineered her history just as she recut the sleeves of a dress: unfastening seams that pinched, cutting unsightly threads, and then sewing it back together.

"Rewrite your life story so that it becomes meaningful—leading to growth and transformation," says Catherine Ann Jones in her book *Heal Your Self with Writing*.

Like stories in books and movies, your life story will have a hero (you), a quest, obstacles to overcome to achieve the story's goal, a climax—and hopefully a happy ending.

Mining for Gold

What's your story?

If your childhood didn't meet your expectations, if your family or personal history feels like a hindrance, or if you are dragging around the baggage of a disappointing, hurtful or traumatic past—*act as if* you had a different past.

Live the life you imagine. Retell your story—leaving out the bits you don't want to relive.

8

TAKE YOUR CHANCE

Go ahead and take chances because that's the only way you're actually gonna find out where your sweet spot is.

—Aaron Sorkin, screenwriter

Multi-millionaire romance author Nora Roberts didn't start out being ambitious. She didn't even dream of being an author.

Trapped by snow one bitter winter, she took a chance on romance and decided to write a novel. Even when her first book was rejected, she knew she had found her passion and purpose with writing.

"Writing makes me happy," she once said. Telling stories nourished something her soul ached for. She found her niche—and the rest was history.

"Before I started writing, you name the craft, I did it. I made my own bread. I made my own jam. I needlepointed. I crocheted. I sewed all my boys' clothes. I sewed my own clothes. I was looking for something. And it was writing. It fed something in me."

Feeding your prosperous mindset is as much about feeding your soul as anything. When you create from your heart you tap into your authentic self, passions collide, and more often than not you find your audience and your sweet spot.

In French, *chance* means "luck." Coco Chanel, one of the world's most enduring fashion icons, deeply believed in the power of luck. Taking chances and following opportunities defined her—even when there was no guarantee of success.

This is the same mindset that has defined many successful authors; including Nora Roberts, J.K. Rowling, James Patterson, and Tim Ferris, to name a few from whom I draw inspiration.

If you want to be a writer, take a chance on writing—write, publish, repeat! Pour your whole soul into your writing projects. Commit to completing your great ideas and sharing your work.

Mining for Gold

Success is defined by the things you say "yes" to. What makes you happy?

What irresistible idea or opportunity could you take a chance on?

What are you willing to try, despite not knowing yet whether you'll fail or succeed?

9

BLOSSOM

Love wins. We know it wins.

~ J.K. Rowling, author

Now is the time for your blossoming. You are entering a fertile period of your life. Focus on your innate creativity and its potency, and watch it rapidly grow!

Nourish what your soul aches for and feed your fertile imagination. Your soul hungers for love and creativity and the manifestation of the beauty in your inner world—to witness it and live it in your physical world, too.

Maintain awareness of how quickly and easily your thoughts and feelings are manifesting into conversations, situations, and responses from the Universe. Pay attention to your intuition, divine creativity, and signs of manifestation. Your intuition is the answer. Intuition feels what your eyes can't see. Trust it.

After years of struggling as a single parent, J.K Rowling hit molten gold when she listened to her intuitive guidance urging her to write a story about a young boy who had magical gifts.

You've heard about the Harry Potter masterpiece, right? What's less known is that she succeeded despite significant odds, including a crippling lack of self-esteem. But she believed in the power of her stories. After Rowling suffered numerous rejections, a publisher finally said "yes" and gave her a small advance of £1500. The publisher advised her to find a daily job because it was very unlikely she'd earn a living from children's books.

But she wrote anyway, and in the process her soul purpose was fertilised and the blossoming of her destiny was assured.

Today, Rowling is one of the wealthiest writers, with major movie adaptations of her books and millions of copies sold worldwide. When people in the publishing industry speak about bestsellers, they use the term "the Harry Potter effect" to describe record sales.

Commit to swiftly becoming that which you choose to think, feel, speak, and believe. Now is the time to align yourself with love, allowing your thoughts to serve you well. The manifestations you set in motion will be ones that enhance your life experience, rather than the current ones you no longer wish to hang on to.

It will require time, habit, and constancy to change patterns of thought and behaviour, but it can be done. Allow yourself absolute and radical permission to detach from past thoughts and actions, to bear the challenge of not knowing who you are, or how you will be on the 'other side' of transformation, in order to let prosperity happen.

Mining for Gold

You are in the midst of change. Let go and enjoy your unfolding.

Pay attention to your intuition, divine creativity, and signs of manifestation. Commit.

CULTIVATE A BURNING DESIRE

10

THE POWER OF PASSION

Of all strata of the pyramid, passion is the most important for your writer's soul and, almost always, your ultimate success.

~ James Scott Bell, author

"Nothing great in the world has been accomplished without passion," the philosopher G.W.F. Hegel once said.

- Passion is energy. Without energy, you have nothing.
- To be passionate is to be fully alive.
- Passion is about emotion, feeling, zest, and enthusiasm.
- Passion is about intensity, fervour, ardour, and zeal.
- Passion is about fire.
- Passion is about eagerness and preoccupation.
- Passion is about excitement and animation.
- Passion is about determination and self-belief.
- Passion, like love and joy, is contagious.
- Passion can't be faked. It's the mark of authenticity.

"What you write becomes who you are ... So make sure you love what you write!" says J.K. Rowling.

Passion fuels inner purpose and fires the flames of your imagination. It gives you a reason for living and the confidence and drive to pursue your dreams. Passion enables you to unleash latent forces and God-given talents.

"We each have passions and skills, but you'll see extraordinarily successful people with one intense emotion or one learned ability that shines through, defining them or driving them more than anything else," writes Gary Keller in *The One Thing: The Surprisingly Simple Truth Behind Extraordinary Results*.

"Often, the line between passion and skills can be blurry. That's because they're almost always connected," Keller says.

When you follow your passion, you'll find your sweet spot. You'll be emboldened by love— thus powering your creativity, courage, resolve, and tenacity, and increasing your likelihood of achieving extraordinary success.

Focus on what excites you. "I find things I like and I do them," says James Patterson, arguably one of the most financially successful authors today.

James Patterson, J.K. Rowling, and other authors have successfully turned their passion for telling stories into a skill, and ultimately a profession, by simply writing.

Mining for Gold

Feel the power that comes from focusing on what excites you.

How can you channel your passions into your writing?
What's your one thing?

11

FIND YOUR PURPOSE

We are all pens in the hands of a writing God sending love letters to the world.

~ Mother Theresa

Many successful authors testify to the power of writing with purpose and sharing their stories and purpose-driven words.

"It is in giving that I connect with others, with the world and with the divine", says author Isabel Allende.

Tapping into higher levels of consciousness is how many prosperous authors of both fiction and non-fiction achieve phenomenal results.

As Dr. Joe Dispenza writes in his book *Evolve Your Brain: The Science of Changing Your Mind*, "An innate higher intelligence gives us life."

Centred around what you may call your divine, spiritual, or subconscious mind, Dispenza's research has shown that when people tap into their inner power they connect with a greater mind and an elevated consciousness.

Others refer to this heightened super-consciousness as their soul or heart, and believe that we are all born into this life with a pre-destined life purpose.

It is in living this soul purpose, and consciously or unconsciously tapping into universal needs, that people forge connections that lead to their prosperity.

Very often the gifts that are bestowed to successful authors arise from some of the darkest nights of their souls. They use their writing to heal and transcend their pain and share what they have learned in the hope that it helps others.

J.K. Rowling escaped an abusive relationship and found comfort creating a fantasy world full of magic.

Elizabeth Gilbert left a loveless marriage and wrote *Eat, Pray, Love*.

Austrian neurologist and psychiatrist Viktor Frankl wrote *Man's Search for Meaning* following his experience as a prisoner in German concentration camps.

Paulo Coelho wrote *The Alchemist* in less than two weeks following his own search for meaning. The book's main theme is about finding one's destiny. According to The New York Times, *The Alchemist* is more self-help than literature.

"When you really want something to happen, the whole universe will conspire so that your wish comes true," an old king tells Santiago in *The Alchemist*. This is the core of the novel's philosophy and a motif that plays throughout Coelho's writing.

He speaks from experience—turning his back on the legal profession his parents wanted him to pursue, Coelho desperately wanted to become a writer.

"Books are not here to show how intelligent and cultivated you are. Books are out there to show your heart, to show your soul, and to tell your fans 'I'm not alone'," Coelho says.

"I hope you are not alone; you can identify yourself with my books, my words, as I can identify myself with your garden, your music—anything we do with love."

BENEFITS OF CREATING with purpose include:

- Tapping into your life's purpose gives you an edge; it stokes the flames of passion, enthusiasm, drive, and initiative needed to succeed
- A sense of purpose can give you the courage, tenacity, and clarity of vision needed to thrive
- Purpose fuels the embers of flagging motivation and latent dreams
- A sense of purpose can lead you to the work you were born to do
- Discovering your true calling opens you up to the dreams the Universe has for you—bigger than you can dream for yourself
- Creating with purpose connects you with divine intelligence, universal energy, and the laws of attraction—magnetising readers to you

MINING FOR GOLD

What experiences give your life meaning and purpose?

How could writing with purpose benefit you and others?

12

A VISION OF VICTORY

If you want to be a millionaire author being an indie romance author is brilliant.

~ Joanna Penn

"Begin with the end in mind," encourages Steven Covey in his runaway bestselling book *The Seven Habits of Highly Successful People*.

Your vision is your "why;" it's the furnace that stokes your desire and fuels your dreams.

What is your vision? What does your prosperous life look like? Is prosperity a passive income that funds your lifestyle? Is it the ability to live and work anywhere in the world? Or is it truckloads of sales on Amazon and buckets of savings in the bank?

Strengthen your vision by clarifying your reasons for wanting to succeed.

"I started to write romance because I needed to make money," says Mary Bly, a tenured professor of English Literature at Fordham

University. Bly writes best-selling Regency and Georgian romance novels under her pen name Eloisa James.

When she first started writing romances, she was struggling to pay back the debt incurred during her professional studies—and was soon hooked.

"You go where your vision is. Think big, feel big, and know in your heart that you are one with God," says Joseph Murphy, Ph.D., author and New Thought minister.

"And you will project a radiance, a glow, a confidence, a joy, and a healing vibration which blesses all who come within your orbit now and forevermore."

Mining for Gold

Define your vision. See it clearly in your mind and heart.

Engage all the senses until it becomes your living reality.

13

DREAM BIG

Don't set out to write a good thriller. Set out to write a #1 thriller.

~James Patterson

Dream big encourages James Patterson, currently the bestselling author in the world. Patterson, whose father was raised in a poorhouse, knows the power of big dreams and passionate perseverance. His first book was turned down by 21 publishers and won The Edgar for Best First Mystery. He also quit a lucrative legal career because it didn't make him bounce.

It's a funny thing, given that science has barely even begun, to explore the real potential of the human mind, how easily we persuade ourselves of its limitations and settle for less.

You've probably caught yourself thinking about a big dream, some inspired course of action, and at some point talked yourself down by saying, "I could never do that!"

Or perhaps you've come up with a bright idea about something and then shelved it because somebody said dismissively, "You can't do that!" or "That's crap."

Or perhaps, as I have so often said to myself before reconnecting with my millionaire mindset, "I can't do this. I can't write this book. It's too big. Who do I think I am trying to write such a complex book?"

But how do you really know what you are capable of unless you try?

Paulo Coehlo, author of *The Alchemist*, once said: "Know what you want and try to go beyond your own expectations. Improve your dancing, practice a lot, and set a very high goal, one that will be difficult to achieve.

"Because that is an artist's million: to go beyond one's limits. An artist who desires very little and achieves it has failed in life."

Thinking big demands a long step outside the comfort zone of what you know.

It can feel scary to contemplate stepping out of the space where you feel you know what you're doing and you feel fully in control.

It can feel frightening to explore what it would be like if you were to leave the comfort rut and attempt to climb toward a new summit. You don't know for sure where it will lead. But everyone who's ever made a success of anything started with a big dream.

And you can, too.

Tim Ferris dreams big by adopting and cherishing his beginner's mind. Rather than succumb to the fear of failure, he changes his mindset and affirms his love of variety and challenge and being a perpetual debutante.

"Think small," encourages Gary Keller in his book *The One Thing*. "Going small" is ignoring all the things you could do and doing what you should do.

"It's recognising that not all things matter equally and finding the things that matter most. It's a tighter way to connect what you do with what you want. It's realising that extraordinary results are directly determined by how narrow you can make a focus."

When you think too big, achieving success can feel overwhelming, time-consuming, and complicated. Calendars can become overloaded and success starts to feel out of reach. So, people opt out and either quit or settle for less.

"Unaware that big success comes when we do a few things well, they get lost trying to do too much, and in the end accomplish too little," says Keller.

"Over time they lower their expectations, abandon their dreams, and allow their life to get small. This is the wrong thing to make small."

Mining for Gold

Every extraordinary achievement starts as someone's daydream. Dream big. Fuel your verve—pursue the vision that sparkles.

Dream big but plan small. Baby steps will lead to bigger success.

Become audaciously obsessed. Anchor your dreams within your heart and feel as though they are already achieved.

14

WHAT MAKES YOU HAPPY?

When I don't write I feel my world shrinking. I feel I am in prison. I feel I lose my fire and my colour. It should be a necessity, and I call it breathing.

~ Anais Nin

As Oprah Winfrey once said, "You know you are on the road to success if you would do your job, and not be paid for it."

When you write with joy, everything is heightened. Your words have spring and bounce, liveliness and vivaciousness—that's why good writing, even if the subject is dark, has longevity. Readers can feel this infectious energy in your books.

Writing is a powerfully transformative mode of self-expression. Not everyone agrees that you need to write with joy. Many authors write to get themselves out of a funk, to manage anxiety, or to write their way out of pain.

"A word is not the same with one writer as with another. One tears it from his guts. The other pulls it out of his overcoat pocket," the French poet Charles Peguy once said.

Some authors believe that to write well they must sit at the keyboard and bleed. This may be more to do with disciplining themselves to sit down and do the work.

But many prosperous authors say that when they enter the energy of their book, they transcend their worldly state of mind and commune with the divine.

"I write because it's fun. Writing is play for me," says James Patterson. "Do not torture yourself. That's how people get blocked."

I write joyfully when I write in 15-minute cycles, and when I write outside in the sun surrounded by the birds and the hills and the trees. I write joyfully when I affirm to myself that I love writing and tell myself that I'm an excellent writer. Sooner or later, even if I'm in a funk, reality catches up!

Mining for Gold

When are the times you feel happy writing?

How can you write more joyfully?

15

IMAGINE BETTER

To create the life of your dreams, the time has come for you to love You. Focus on Your joy. Do all the things that make You feel good. Love You, inside and out. Everything will change in your life, when you change the inside of you. Allow the Universe to give you every good thing you deserve, by being a magnet to them all. To be a magnet for every single thing you deserve, you must be a magnet of love.

~ Rhonda Byrne, author

No doubt you've heard the saying, "Out of sight, out of mind." But what, if anything, are you doing to keep your dream of making a living from your writing visible?

"What practical strategies are you going to implement as a result of reading this book?" I wrote to an advance reader.

Her reply was, "Drawing/painting and writing all the things I have in my mind about my project. Getting my specific passion journal that is solely for my new project out and having it constantly with me, feeding it every day."

In my book *How to Find Your Passion and Purpose*, I share tips and links to help you create a passion journal. Another variation of this is to create a prosperity dream board. This is where manifesting your preferred future really happens.

I have covered the wall of my writing room with images of the books I have written and plan to write, feedback from people who have encouraged me on my writer's journey, and feeling-based images of what prosperity means to me—including a photo of me and my partner on vacation (feeling awesome, happy, and free).

Every time I sit in my writing chair looking at my prosperity board, it is a motivational kick-start; a feeling-based affirmation of not only what I yearn for, but the successes I have already manifested.

So many things I've visualised and affirmed on my prosperity board are now my living realities. And the others? I have no doubt that they soon will be!

"If you think vision boards are bogus, then the joke's on you. They work, and there's actually a really simple explanation of why they work so well," writes Elizabeth Rider in *The Huffington Post*.

"Creating a sacred space that displays what you want actually does bring it to life. What we focus on expands. When you create a vision board and place it in a space where you see it often, you essentially end up doing short visualisation exercises throughout the day."

Visualisation is one of the most powerful mind exercises you can do.

"The law of attraction is forming your entire life experience and it is doing that through your thoughts. When you are visualising, you are emitting a powerful frequency out into the Universe," writes Rhonda Byrne in her popular book *The Secret*.

Whether you believe that or not, we know that visualisation works. As Rider writes in her article "Olympic athletes have been using it for decades to improve performance, and *Psychology Today* reported that the brain patterns activated when a weightlifter lifts heavy weights are also similarly activated when the lifter just imagined (visualised) lifting weights."

. . .

Brain Gym

In the traditions of Napoleon Hill, Earl Nightingale and Maxwell Maltz, author Jack Canfield also emphasises the importance of focusing on a vision and creating compelling and vivid pictures in your mind in order to achieve your goals. Canfield cites neuropsychologists who study expectancy theory to support his view on the significance of visualisation.

Scientists once believed that people responded to information flowing into the brain from the outside world. But today, they've figured out that we respond to what the brain, based on prior experiences, expects to happen next.

Scientists have discovered that the mind is such a powerful instrument, it can deliver literally everything you want.

But you must believe that what you want is possible...

This is where visualisation works its magic. Seeing is believing! By programming your brain to expect that something will happen a certain way, you achieve exactly what you anticipate.

How do you create a vision or prosperity board that works? It's simple: Your vision board should focus on how you want, or expect, to *feel*. Because you're aiming for prosperity, you'll *expect* to feel great! So, be sure to evoke these feelings on your prosperity wall.

MINING FOR GOLD

Manifest your preferred future—imagine better by bringing your vision of prosperity into being.

It doesn't have to be a wall—it could be a poster board you can move around. Or, as my partner and I once did when visualising the million-dollar property we dreamed of buying (and later purchased), you can create a manifestation fridge!

16

PROTECT YOUR DREAM

We celebrate success, but I think we should also just celebrate giving it a go.

~ Phil Keoghan, television personality

In the movie *The Pursuit of Happiness*, Will Smith, who plays the role of a homeless man, says to his son, "You got a dream, you gotta protect it. People can't do something themselves, they wanna tell you that you can't do it. You want something? Go get it. Period."

People who are impatient to see the realisation of your dreams may say, "Show me the money," "You've left it too late," or some other "downer" message.

Ignore them.

"It's already been done," people said to Tim Ferris when he shared his idea of starting a podcast. Instead of letting others talk him out of starting his show, he did it anyway.

His podcast is now ranked as the #1 business podcast on all of iTunes. It was the first business/interview podcast to pass 100,000,000 downloads. It was also selected as iTunes' "Best of 2014" and "Best of 2015." Tim Ferris has also been called "the Oprah of radio."

"Always believe in your work—it will carry you through any difficult situation, but learn to adjust your thinking every once in a while to fit the moment. Never give up. You won't always get everything right every time—but you have to keep trying. Have the commitment to persevere," architect Dame Zaha Mohammad Hadid once said.

If Hadid's wise words of encouragement could have reached F. Scott Fitzgerald, and others like him who have been plagued by critics, the world would be made richer.

As Jeff Goins writes in *Real Artists Don't Starve: Timeless Strategies for Thriving in the New Creative Age*, in 1923, when Fitzgerald began writing his third novel, the author was feeling supremely confident. "'Artistically,' he wrote in a letter to his editor, Max Perkins, 'it's head [and] shoulders over everything I've done.'"

But the more he worked, the more self-conscious he grew. As the new novel approached publication, Fitzgerald grew nervous. "'*The Great Gatsby* is weak,' he said of the title, casting his vote instead for *On the Road to West Egg* or *The High-Bouncing Lover*.

Fitzgerald worried the book wouldn't appeal to women, that the reviews would be bad, and that it wouldn't sell well enough to pay the publisher back his advance.

"As Fitzgerald expected, almost all these fears came true. *The Great Gatsby* was published on April 10, 1925, with one New York paper headlining its review: 'F. Scott Fitzgerald's Latest a Dud.'

"The rest of the literary world was equally critical, with H. L. Mencken calling it 'no more than a glorified anecdote' and referring to the author as 'this clown.'

"A bit more bluntly, Ruth Snyder wrote, 'We are quite convinced after reading *The Great Gatsby* that Mr. Fitzgerald is *not* one of the great American writers of today.'

"*Gatsby* did not achieve the success its author had hoped for, selling fewer than half as many copies as any of his previous novels. The failure crushed him."

He died in 1940 at the age of forty-four regarding himself as a failure. However, the novel experienced a revival during World War II, and became a part of American high school curricula and numerous stage and film adaptations in the following decades.

In 2013, the book was again adapted into a movie, and today *The Great Gatsby* is widely considered a literary classic and a contender for the title "Great American Novel"—something Fitzgerald dreamed of achieving but died disbelieving.

Mining for Gold

Set your horizons high, believe in the beauty of your dreams and don't settle for less. Go for it—try!

How can you protect your dreams and strengthen your ability to persevere?

17

FIND YOUR VIBE TRIBE

When you choose to step out of limiting thoughts and listen to the song in your heart, you'll find the people who want to share and celebrate the journey with you. You'll find your tribe.

~ Dr. Julie Connor, author

The simplest definition of a tribe is a group of people that share the same language, customs, beliefs—and aspirations.

As you've already discovered, sometimes to flourish you need to break free of your current tribe and find one that fuels your dreams and brings out the best in you.

Your vibe tribe is a great team of others—whether they be significant friends, partners, or family members, or those found online through wonderful Facebook groups and webinars.

Gathering a team of like-minded people will nourish your burning desire and elevate your success.

I found my author vibe tribe online. We have never met in person, but we stay connected and share success strategies via Facebook, and occasionally we link-up on video conferencing calls.

As I write this chapter, a member of my vibe tribe, Scott Allen, who is the author of many brilliant books about living fearlessly, sent me a PDF of his successful book launch strategy. This is a powerful example of being co-creators in one another's mutual success.

My vibe tribe also finds me—reaching out to me after enjoying my books. Many of my readers love to help me co-create prosperity by reading advance copies of my new books and contributing valuable feedback.

This feedback, and the positive reviews on Amazon and via the online communities I have created for my readers on Facebook, sustains me and encourages me to keep writing. I love hearing their success stories.

Other readers have helped me grow my vibe tribe by interviewing me on their podcasts and success summits. Recently, Sheree Clark, a fabulous and influential healthy-living coach based in the US, discovered my book *Mid-life Career Rescue: The Call for Change* and showcased it on American television. She also included an interview with me in her fabulous "What the Fork" summit. You'll find a link to this interview and the TV clip on my media page at www.cassandragaisford.com/media.

Successful authors and podcasters like Tim Ferris (tim.blog/podcast) and Joanna Penn (www.thecreativepenn.com) found their vibe tribes by following their enthusiasms. They created their vibes by following their passionate purposes to share what they learn with others.

Here's a few ways to find a vibe tribe:

- Scan Facebook for like-minded groups
- Enrol in a writing course—they often include a private members group on social media
- Create a Facebook community of your own—show up and encourage others
- Listen to podcasts which inspire you to become the best

version of you—Joanna Penn's podcast is very helpful for "'authorpreneurs." I also love Neil Patel's podcast for savvy marketing strategies: http://neilpatel.com/podcast. Tim Ferriss' podcast is also always inspiring http://tim.blog/podcast.
- Join writers' groups and become an active member of writing bodies—romance writers, for example, gain huge encouragement from The Romance Writers of America, Australia and New Zealand. These professional groups are dedicated to helping their members thrive. They offer courses to learn new skills from established authors; the chance to enter competitions where you can gain valuable feedback (or win!); conferences at which to network, meet agents and pitch your books—and much more encouragement
- Check out Meetup.com and find a group of like-mined souls to meet up with in person
- Speak from your heart, write with passion and purpose, and send your love letters to the world via your books, blogs, podcasts, or other mediums, including social media

Mining for Gold

How can you develop an encouraging network of friends and acquaintances?

How can you remove yourself from people who don't encourage or support your dreams?

Finish your writing project and get your book out there—magnetise your vibe tribe to you.

18

CREATE A NEW DESTINY

The 5 percent of your mind that is conscious was fighting against the 95 percent that is the subconscious body-mind. Thinking one way and feeling another cannot produce anything tangible.

~ Dr. Joe Dispenza, author

"Becoming a new personality produces a new reality," writes Dr. Joe Dispenza in his book *Breaking Free of Being You*.

"Simply said, you can't create a new person, a new reality, while you are being the old personality."

If your current personality, how you think, feel, and act, is creating experiences that you're not happy with, if your results aren't at the level you'd like, if you're not thrilled with who you are and who you've become, create a new self—and a new reality.

Many successful authors who have created pen names know the power of changing their identities.

Your creativity and ability to recreate your reality is one of your most powerful gifts. Your goal of creating a new destiny may require forging a new personality and a new state of being—complete with new, more empowering thoughts, feelings, and actions.

It won't happen overnight. But, just like an actor rehearsing for a major role, with practice you can shed your old identity. No longer emotionally chained to known situations in your life that keep recycling the same circumstances, you free yourself to reinvent your life.

If this is a strategy that appeals to you, I highly recommend purchasing a copy of *Breaking Free of Being You*. Here are just a few of the many simple but powerful strategies you will need to use to reinvent yourself:

1.) Craft the specific future events you want to experience by observing them into physical reality. Let yourself go and begin to free-associate without analysis. The pictures you see in your mind are the vibrational blueprints of your new destiny. You, as the quantum observer, are commanding matter to conform to your intentions.

2.) Give up trying to figure out how or when or where or with whom. Leave those details to a mind that knows so much more than you do. And know that your creation will come in a way that you will least expect, that will surprise you and leave no doubt that it came from a higher order. Trust that the events in your life will be tailored to your conscious intentions.

3.) Mentally rehearse the new you. Create in your mind's eye how you want to live your life. Move into a new state of being; change your mind and think in new ways. Live in the emotions of a new future. Pick a potential in the quantum field and live it completely. Remember who and what you really are in your new future.

You may find, as I did when I completed this exercise and others in Joe Dispenza's book, that your intuition guides you and provides clear insight.

When I thought of who I was in my new reality, James Patterson came to mind. I thought, if I was James Patterson how would I act? How would I start my day? How would I feel? What would I say?

James Patterson turned his back on a lucrative career that no longer fulfilled him. He is wealthy, prolific, and diverse. He writes in a variety of genres, thrives in the area of writing snappy short chapters, and is incredibly generous with his wealth. Patterson is also highly committed to having fun.

This all sounds good to me. Using Patterson, and others I admire, I have a helpful template to begin creating an enhanced personality—including adopting more 'masculine' traits such as single-mind focus. In this way I bring balance to the female energy that I also value and honour.

I may even experiment with a gender-neutral pen name such as C.G. Ford. Romance writer Nora Roberts achieved a successful genre shift when she wrote her thrillers as J.D. Robb.

While I'm on this topic, I also wonder whether Joanne Rowling would have achieved the same success if she hadn't hidden her name and her gender by writing as J.K. Rowling? I also find it fascinating that she chose to write a new series under the pseudonym Robert Galbraith—not Roberta or Robyn or another woman's name.

Mining for Gold

What parts of your personality propel you toward prosperity? What thoughts, feelings, and actions need to change?

Create your new personality—change how you think, feel, and act. Borrow from people you admire if this helps the co-creation process.

19

MAKE SPACE FOR PROSPERITY

#1 prosperity secret—you need to make space for it!

~ Colette Baron-Reid, author

"Be ruthless about protecting writing days, i.e., do not cave in to endless requests to have 'essential' and 'long overdue' meetings on those days," advises J.K. Rowling.

"The funny thing is that, although writing has been my actual job for several years now, I still seem to have to fight for time in which to do it.

"Some people do not seem to grasp that I still have to sit down in peace and write the books, apparently believing that they pop up like mushrooms without my connivance.

"I must therefore guard the time allotted to writing as a Hungarian Horntail guards its firstborn egg."

Whether it's making space to create, or clearing room to allow prosperity into your life, it's going to take fierce determination from you to give birth to your dreams—mentally, emotionally, and spiritually.

Being fierce doesn't need to be aggressive; it's simply an unwavering commitment to protect your burning desire. As Steven Covey wrote in his book *The Seven Habits of Highly Effective People*, very often the things that matter most are downgraded to non-urgent. Instead, the seemingly urgent, but truly unimportant, things crowd in and take centre stage.

When this happens, you'll find inspiration quickly turning to despair, frustration, and despondency. Who will be to blame?

You will.

Before you protest and fire a round of excuses and justifications, I can tell you I've heard them all—because I've said them all.

"My daughter needs me. My partner needs me. My friend wants to call around. I feel guilty. I need a coffee"—or something similar. Excuses, excuses, and more excuses.

Prioritise your creativity. It's that simple—and at times it's that challenging. Isolate the barriers, blocks, whatever is standing in the way.

Here's a few of the ways I've tamed my excuses and created space for prosperity:

- Meditating daily
- Being scheduled with my writing time—mornings are my most productive time
- Listening to blogs and podcast interviews of prosperous authors
- Tapping into my love of variety and creating writing rooms —the garden shed, the local cafe, sitting in the herb garden overlooking the sea
- Journaling for prosperity
- Writing Morning Pages and using oracle cards to clear away funk and improve my mood
- Removing myself from negativity and distracting people

- Prioritising my health and creating harmonious relationships
- Hypnosis and tapping into my superconscious
- Reading books about prosperity
- Letting go—surrendering versus stressful striving
- Eliminating stress and committing to daily practices that elevate my energy levels
- Enlisting those closest to me to help by honouring and respecting my need to make space for prosperity

IF MORNING PAGES are a new concept to you, I explain this wonderful tool (developed by Julia Cameron, author of *The Artist's Way*) a little more in the chapter "Journal Your Way to Success," and also on my blog here: www.cassandragaisford.com/making-space-for-prosperity/.

MINING FOR GOLD

How can you create space for prosperity? What do you need to do more of, less of, start doing, or stop doing?

How important is peace, tranquility, and harmony to you? What needs to change to bring these qualities into greater alignment?

How assertive are you? Master the art of saying "no."

Take an inventory of opportunities and threats and then commit to problem-solving.

Intensify your desire, remind yourself of your "why." What benefits will flow?

How will you feel if you fail to make space for prosperity?

DIVE DEEPER...

In 2017, I was interviewed by Courtney Kennedy for her fabulous book *Creating Space to Thrive: Get Unstuck, Reboot Your Creativity and Change Your Life*. You can read an edited excerpt and find a link to her book on my blog here: www.cassandragaisford.com/creating-space-to-thrive-get-unstuck-reboot-your-creativity-and-change-your-life/.

Be inspired by other people who have made the leap to creativity—people like Coco Chanel and Leonardo da Vinci. Read their stories and learn the secrets to their success in my *The Art of Success* series. Available now from all good online retailers.

TURNING PRO

20

REALITY CHECK

Show me the money!

~ Cuba Gooding Jr., in Jerry Maguire

As Joanna Penn writes in her book *How to Make a Living with Your Writing*, "A survey in *The Guardian UK* in April 2015 stated that the median earnings of professional authors fall below the minimum wage.

"The bottom 50% of UK authors made less than £10,500 in 2013 (around US $16,000). It's often reported that the average book will sell fewer than 500 copies, which of course, is not enough for a sustainable income. The top 5% are making more than that."

Yes, people do make a living from their writing, a very good living, but the reality is that many people don't. You'll find it a lot easier to manage your mindset if you start honestly.

Deluding yourself with an excess of sunny optimism and dreams of getting rich quick will increase anxiety, despondency, and despair.

Ultimately, you'll be discouraged from persevering with your goal of making an extraordinary living with your writing.

But a healthy reality check doesn't need to be a deterrent to building a successful writing career. Armed with the facts, you can develop a strategy to increase your odds of success.

Pursuing several careers at once might seem crazy, but not only is it a growing trend, for some—especially as they start out— it's the only way to earn money doing what they love.

James Patterson kept his day job as a lawyer and penned crime novels on the side. He now writes in a variety of genres, and has mastered the art of writing short, impactful books which satisfy his voracious readers.

Author C.J. Lyons continued to work as a paramedic while building her career writing thrillers. She said it took seven books before she started to see a regular income stream.

Mary Bly enjoys her salaried position as a tenured professor of English Literature while penning Regency and Georgian romance novels under her pen name, Eloisa James.

Nicholas Sparks was turned down by over 25 agents and was on the verge of bankruptcy when he hit it big with *The Notebook*. The manuscript was sold for 1 million dollars and was quickly made into the movie we all know and love.

J.K. Rowling lived in near poverty as a single mother on benefits and endured similar rejections before she hit the jackpot.

MINING FOR GOLD

How can you follow your passion and still pay the bills?

You'll find more suggestions to help you finance your career in the section "Slaying Obstacles," and also in my book *Mid-Life Career Rescue: Employ Yourself*.

21

UNDERSTAND THE RULES

Rules are what makes art beautiful.

~ Aaron Sorkin, screenwriter

If you want to fast-track your success in any endeavour you need to understand the tried-and-proven rules of your chosen field.

"Writing is like any other art form, there are chunks of it that can be taught, and there are chunks of it that can't . . . we're here for the parts that can be taught," says screenwriter Aaron Sorkin.

Dismiss the idea that art is not a place for rules. I like to think of rules as tried and tested principles that are proven to work.

You can fan your true burning desire for prosperity and make an extraordinary living from your writing by learning from your heroes.

Who do you admire? Who has achieved the prosperity you yearn for? What rules do they follow? Become a diagnostician and analyse their success strategy.

Learn those rules by watching films, reading screenplays,

studying novels, and taking them apart and putting them back together.

When something doesn't work, figure out why it doesn't work. Did it break one of the rules?

Similarly, when you analyse what rules others are applying as part of their success strategies, highlight the tools and methods you aren't using, and ask yourself, "Why aren't I doing this?"

Consider revisiting your strategy and applying a new approach. I did this recently when I noticed that many authors were successfully using Amazon ads to market their books. Incorporating this into my marketing efforts was relatively easy and yielded a dramatic increase in sales.

Increasing your income definitely improves your mindset!

Mining for Gold

What rules and principles do you need to learn and what do you need to break?

Keep a journal and write down what works about your five favourite books or movies and what doesn't work about your five least favourite books or movies.

Repeat this analysis with any other approach you wish to learn—including mindset strategies, marketing, and book promotion activities.

We'll dive deeper into promotion strategies in book three of *The Prosperity for Authors* series—*Creating Soaring Profits.*

22

DAILY HABITS

A writer who waits for ideal conditions under which to work will die without putting a word on paper.

~ E.B. White

"We often assume that great things are done by those who were blessed with natural talent, genius, and skill. But how many great things could have been done by people who never fully realised their potential?" writes James Clear on his popular blog.

How can you pull your potential from within and share it with the world? By doing the work!

Professional authors have found that creating and committing to productive daily routines maximises their output and minimises their stress.

"Success is nothing more than a few simple disciplines practiced every day," says author Jim Rohn.

"Top performers in any field, including writing, tap into something that goes much deeper than intelligence or talent. They possess an obsessive devotion to do the work that needs to be done," Rohn says.

James Clear recently profiled a few masters of their daily routines on his blog:

Novelist Haruki Murakami says, "The repetition itself becomes the important thing." He gets up at four a.m. and works for five to six hours. No excuses. "I keep to this routine every day without variation," he says.

"I write every morning," said Ernest Hemingway. "When I am working on a book or a story I write every morning as soon after first light as possible."

"There is no one to disturb you and it is cool or cold and you come to your work and warm as you write. You read what you have written and, as you always stop when you know what is going to happen next, you go on from there."

In 1932, the famous writer and painter Henry Miller created a work schedule that listed his "Commandments" for him to follow as part of his daily routine. This list was published in his book, *Henry Miller on Writing*.

Several of Miller's tips that resonated with me include:

1. Work on one thing at a time until finished
2. Start no more new books, add no more new material
3. Don't be nervous. Work calmly, joyously, recklessly on whatever is at hand
4. Work according to Program and not according to mood. Stop at the appointed time!
5. Keep human! See people, go places, drink if you feel like it
6. Don't be a draught-horse! Work with pleasure only

SOME OF THE many daily habits I schedule include regular meditation, Morning Pages, and writing first thing in the morning until 12. These routines and the many other little things I regularly do, when taken together, make an extraordinary difference to my energy levels and productivity.

Mining for Gold

What daily habits and routines would make a tremendous difference to your mindset?

23

FILL A NEED

If you want to be a commercial writer, write what people want to read.

~ Marissa Peer, hypnotherapist & author

In a 2017 *New York Times* cover story, psychotherapist and author Esther Perl was called the most important game changer in sexuality and relational health since famous sex therapist Dr. Ruth. "Her ideas are like the chorus of a really good pop song—instantly familiar because they resonate deeply," *The Observer* wrote.

Everything Esther commits to is driven by her purpose to help fill arguably one of the greatest needs in society today—connection. "Nothing will give us more meaning in life than to know that we matter for others," she recently said on the *Tim Ferris Show*.

With her passion for improving relationships and the way intimate partners connect, Perl has channeled her professional expertise as a couples' counsellor into her books, and has authored international bestsellers, including *Mating in Captivity*.

Successful romance authors, such as Nora Roberts, also fill a need

—the need to escape reality and enter an enchanted world of hope, empowerment, and happily-ever-after's. "I'm not loved, but when I read a romance I feel loved," a reader once shared.

Marissa Peer was named Best British Therapist by *Men's Health Magazine* and has made a name for herself writing weight-loss books and producing self-empowerment products—including hypnosis audios.

"I have a gift. I can tell what's wrong with a person in three minutes and cure them in five," she once said.

I wrote my range of self-empowerment books, including *Mid-Life Career Rescue (The Call For Change): How to Confidently Leave a Job You Hate and Start Living a Life You Love, Before It's Too Late*, to help encourage mature workers to leave jobs that were slowly killing them and to strive to live their best lives.

These books filled a demographical need of an ageing population and workforce faced with economic shifts caused by the ever-diminishing government superannuation.

MINING FOR GOLD

What social, demographic, economic, or future needs could your writing help solve?

24

FINISH WHAT YOU START

Whatever I'm doing I get very guilty if I don't put a good day's work in. I'm not one for making excuses. I had this Catholic upbringing. I was taught to finish what you start.

~ Nora Roberts, author

Nothing improves your mindset more than a sense of achievement. The opposite is also true—leaving projects unfinished fuels feelings of failure.

Leaving tasks hanging increases anxiety, depression, and feelings of unworthiness. Don't do this to yourself.

I know how destructive this can be to your confidence—and success. For years I had half-written manuscripts clogging up my mind and computer.

People around me began to get frustrated, annoyed, and cross. My cheerleaders began to give up on me. I almost gave up on myself. Finally, in my fifties, I channeled this horrendous frustration into finishing my books. One of my helpful enabling mantras was, "Done is better than perfect."

I published three non-fiction books in four months—all of them shot to #1 on Amazon. You can do this! In Book Two of the *Prosperity for Authors* series, you'll learn powerhouse productivity tools you can harness to help you finish what you start.

What's important now is devotion. Devote yourself to the energy of your book. Devote yourself to the inspiration that planted the fire in your belly. Devote yourself to completing your books.

A devoted person is a loyal person.

As playwright and novelist Henry Miller once said, "Start no more new books, add no more new material to existing books. Work on one thing at a time until finished."

Your reward for finishing your book, as is mine, will be the satisfaction of seeing your baby fly into the world, and the joy of having space to give birth to a new book.

Learn how to "knock the bugger off" in the next chapter! It's a super inspiring story to encourage us all to persevere with our dreams.

Mining for Gold

How can you pour your whole soul into your writing projects?

How can you become devoted to finishing your books and increase your ability to complete your projects? What do you need to do more or less of, start doing, or stop doing?

25

KNOCK THE BUGGER OFF

Giving up on telling this story was never an option for me.

~ Heather Morris, author

This is a longer chapter than my earlier ones, but this following success story is too inspiring to cut short.

I first met Heather Morris when she came to the Bay of Islands in New Zealand from her home in Melbourne to visit her brother, and my friend, who had been given a terminal diagnosis of cancer.

As you can appreciate, this was a very distressing time. Yet, as we discovered we all had a passion for telling stories, and as we shared our writing inspiration, we all felt encouraged, emboldened, and filled with light.

And with this came renewed hope.

Not just for her brother, who was inspired to crack on with his own writing projects, but I was also reminded of the finality of life. This provided added motivation to crack on with my own writing projects.

For a small moment in time, we all escaped our worldly concerns and became excited by Heather's "overnight" (*not!*) success with the publication and resulting worldwide interest in her novel, *The Tattooist of Auschwitz* (to be released in 2018).

The novel is based on the true story of Slovakian Jew Lale Sokolov, who was forced to tattoo the numbers on his fellow victims' arms that would mark them for survival.

Sokolov used the infinitesimal freedom of movement that his position gave him to exchange jewels and money taken from murdered Jews for food to keep others alive. *The Tattooist of Auschwitz* is also a remarkable love story.

"My book is the true story of the girl he fell in love with when he held her hand and tattooed a number on her left arm, and how they survived for two and a half years in that Dante-esque circle of hell, got separated, found each other, married, and lived very happily for over 50 years, " Heather told me.

I invited Heather to share her story and she generously emailed me the following:

I met Lale Sokolov in December 2003. I was 50-years old and had been dabbling in learning and writing screenplays; he was 87-years-old and his wife, Gita, had died two months earlier.

A friend of a friend of their son, Gary, asked me to meet Lale to hear the secret he'd kept for over fifty years and which he wanted to tell someone before he 'hurried up and joined his beloved Gita.'

Over the next three years, our friendship grew as, slowly, his story was revealed to me piecemeal, often told at bullet pace with limited coherency and with no flow or connection to the many, many stories he told.

It didn't matter. I fell under his spell.

Was it the delightful Eastern European accent? Was it the charm this old rascal had lived his life dispensing? Or, was it the twisted, convoluted story I was starting to make sense of—the significance and importance of which was beginning to dawn on me.

It was all of these things and more. I was spending time with 'living history' and was being given a story to tell for which I am honoured and privileged to have been entrusted with.

Fast forward to 2017—14 years after my fateful meeting with Lale Sokolov. It took me two years to get the story I would eventually write into a screenplay. He got to read it and loved it.

I sat with him and held his hand and said goodbye to him the night he died. At that time, I vowed to never stop trying to tell his story.

A film production company optioned the script from me for three years, then another two years, but failed to 'get it up'.

I took the option back and, after a rewrite, started entering it in screenplay competitions around the world. It did well, and was often a finalist and won the International Independent Film Award in 2016.

I was receiving comments from film executives that the story 'not only should be told, but must be told;' that it was 'Oscar bait'. But still no-one came forward to talk production.

Then a light-bulb moment came when I decided to write it as a novel, something I had no experience with and had never written or studied as a writing medium.

On the advice of one of my sons to help with 'free promotion,' I did a Kickstarter campaign to raise funds to self-publish. From this campaign, a local publishing company in Melbourne approached me and signed me up.

I attempted to write while working full-time in a large Melbourne hospital and being the accommodating grandmother to my son and his wife, my daughter and her husband and their three little ones.

I was getting no-where.

I'm lucky to have family living in San Diego, California, who have a holiday house on the top of Big Bear Mountain. In the middle of their winter, in six feet of snow, I squirrelled myself away for four weeks and as Sir Edmund Hilary once said, 'knocked the bugger off.'

The parent company of my publisher came to Melbourne in February and heard about my story. They have now taken over the publishing, sold foreign language rights to 13 countries, and done a deal with Harper Collins in the U.S. to publish there.

And the screenplay? Stay tuned—some heavy hitters in Hollywood are vying for it.

I am now 64 years old and about to embark on a journey beyond my wildest dreams as I travel promoting the book and hopefully, in two or three years' time, a film.

Giving up on telling this story was never an option for me. Yes, months went by when I did nothing to further it as life got in the way. I told myself it was *The Tattooist*'s time, I had to hang in there, seek out avenues to have the story heard and eventually one paid off.

I don't kid myself that I'm a great writer. I am privileged to have been given a great story to tell and I hope Lale and Gita would be proud of the job I've done telling their story. I have received the ultimate validation of my attempt from their son who doesn't want a word changed.

A lot of very talented people/editors both in Melbourne and London will produce a book which I am honoured to have my name on. My family keep telling me they wouldn't be doing that if I hadn't written it in the first place.

I have two quotes on the wall near my desk, the one mentioned above by Sir Edmund and one from one of my favourite screenwriters, William Goldman, who references the children's book *The Little Engine That Could*.

'Just get the @#%&% engine over the mountain.'

As we go to print, Harper Collins has come on board as the publisher in the U.S. and Canada, and major film companies are bidding for the movie rights. Stay tuned!

HEATHER'S STORY is a powerful reminder not to give up on your dreams. Tenacity, perseverance, patience, and the ability to adapt are big factors in her success—and many other attributes as well, including talent!

She began with a film script and then taught herself how to turn a script into a novel. She also taught herself to fund her dreams via the Internet—and then opportunity came knocking. But, importantly, success came because she put her work out there.

It's a reminder to us all that you grow into your dreams, and a commitment to continual learning is essential. As is hanging onto a success mindset.

As Heather said, giving up on telling this story was never an option for her. Heather also proves what Napoleon Hill so famously wrote in his classic book *Think and Grow Rich*—most people don't achieve their success until their sixties and beyond.

Winners never quit and quitters never win, Heather's brother John Williamson, a screen-writer, told me.

Mining for Gold

Brainstorm or list as many ways as possible that you could finance your career. Seek suggestions from others to widen the possibilities. Ask your way to success.

Which of Heather's success strategies could you experiment with? Going AWOL? Learning a new skill? Crowdfunding? Affirmations on the wall—or something else?

Check out Heather's KickStarter Campaign here—www.kickstarter.com/projects/thetattooist/the-tattooist

26

SHOW YOUR WORK

Why would you stop yourself from having the thing we all want in life which is connection.

~ Marissa Peer, hypnotherapist & author

It's great to finish what you start, but even more empowering and courageous, to show your work to people who may be able to help you take it to a wider audience.

"Years ago, I met the person who wrote *Desperate Housewives* and had put it in the drawer for 10 years," writes celebrity hypnotherapist and author Marissa Peer.

Why don't people show their work? Lack of faith, low self-belief, devaluing of their work, and a crippling fear of rejection are very common obstacles to success. Or perhaps you've let the critics stop you.

"When someone wrote *The Sopranos* they said that would never sell. It's not funny and it's violent and it became the most popular show in its demograph," says Peer.

Take a leap of faith. Persevere. If it doesn't work, at least you'll know you gave it your best shot.

As you read in Heather's story, it's amazing how many people were "discovered" when they shared their work.

Mining for Gold

Develop a list of people you could show your work to? This may include a feedback group or critique partners, entering a competition, sharing some excerpts on a public forum, sending your manuscript to a top literary agent, or self-publishing.

27

WRITE WITH CONFIDENCE

Confidence is terribly important for a writer.
You have to write with confidence.

~ Aaron Sorkin, screenwriter

Always write with conviction, or just do it scared—even if you have to fake it to feel it.

Marissa Peer thought she had buckets of confidence until she tackled writing her first book.

"There's three things you need to know about the mind," she said. "It only does what it thinks you want it to do; it responds to the pictures in your head and the words you say to yourself; and it likes what is familiar."

Plagued with doubts and noticing how negative self-talk was sabotaging her progress, she reprogrammed her mindset with empowering self-talk. Some of the things she programmed into her subconscious were the affirmations below:

"This book is brilliant."

"I love writing."

"I love this book."

Marissa knows from her work with clients as a hypnotherapist that the only thing that's stopping you is the fear that you might be rejected.

"But no one can reject you unless you let them. And that's the worst kind, rejecting yourself," she says.

"We know that the major cause of depression is harsh, hurtful, critical words that you say to yourself."

"Therefore, maybe elation is caused by being positive, and complementary and wonderful about yourself and your work and your talents.

"Turn it around. Tell yourself amazing things. If the Universe gave you a writing skill, it will support you in everything—you may have to work at it, but someone gave you that skill. They didn't give Beyoncé that voice so she could sit at home and be a typist."

Whether you fake it or believe it, whatever your approach, back yourself completely—even if it means a willingness to confidently write badly.

Mining for Gold

Say wonderful things out loud about yourself and your writing before, and as, you write.

Intensify your positive feelings with music and moving your body around to get your joy hormones flowing. Screenwriter Aaron Sorkin says this strategy is brilliant.

Join the big CON—write with confidence. Fake it to make it!

Dive deeper…

If your confidence and self-esteem could benefit from an additional boost consider purchasing my book *Boost Your Self-Esteem and Confi-*

dence: Six Easy Steps to Increase Self-Confidence, Self-esteem, Self-Value and Love Yourself More.

Sign up to my *Prosperity for Authors* newsletter to be the first to know when my guided meditations and self-hypnosis audios are released, and stay tuned for news of my *Prosperity for Authors* courses and webinars.
Sign up here http://eepurl.com/bEArfT

PLAN FOR SUCCESS

Do the one thing you think you cannot do. Fail at it. Try again. Do better the second time. The only people who never tumble are those who never mount the high wire. This is your moment. Own it.

~ Oprah

"Luck is preparation meeting opportunity," Oprah once said. Planning and effort prevents poor performance. This is such a powerful message when it comes to your goals, especially if you're someone who equates planning with feeling controlled.

You may be like many people who look to the future thinking, "Someday! Someday I will achieve that."

How can you be assured that things will happen if you don't plan your action steps effectively, efficiently, and productively?

So many people end their lives disappointed that things didn't come to fruition. "Why didn't it happen for me?" they say. "My life is a life of regret."

Successful people don't sit at home waiting for things to happen. They go out and conquer things.

If you're sitting back waiting for "someday" you have a problem—you think you have time!

What is your current planning mindset? Do you plan your life by:

Beginning with the end in mind—planning at least five to ten years ahead, and working back from there to ensure that everything you do now moves you ahead?

Creating outcome-focused goals? Or do you get bogged down in rigidly planning every minute step you must make to achieve the changes, instead of trusting you will figure it out, or trusting the Universe or providence to deliver?

There's a time for planning and a time to create, seize, and act upon opportunities.

It's a balancing act. Whatever your approach, plan to make your success a reality. Your efforts will be repaid in exchange for your labor and your commitment to plan and persevere.

Mining for Gold

Set one goal for yourself and start breaking it down into bite-size chunks. If you want to generate $100,000 from your writing in a year, what do you need to do to get there?

If you want to finish a book, or start a new one, or improve the sales of one you've already published, develop your success strategy.

29
MAINTAIN YOUR FAITH

Faith in action is love.

~ Mother Theresa

As Adam Markel writes in his book *Pivot: The Art and Science of Reinventing Your Career and Life*, "Just because you can't see the steps doesn't mean they aren't there. There's a word for this type of behaviour. It's called faith."

I've always loved the saying, "Faith is the bird that sings in the dark." The challenge and reality about creating a living from your writing is that you never know when, or if, you'll make it big.

Who could have predicted, for example, that the poorly written, badly edited erotic novel *Fifty Shades of Grey*, written by British author E.L. James, would top bestseller lists around the world?

Julia Cameron, an active artist and author of *The Artist's Way* and another thirty or so fiction and non-fiction books, advocates relinquishing too much effort, and instead turning your energy from stressful striving into cultivating faith and trust.

Prayer, gratitude, acceptance, and unwavering belief that everything happens for a reason are just some of the many strategies she encourages people to embrace.

Keep your faith strong by reminding yourself of your purpose, staying positive, and keeping away from cynics.

MINING FOR GOLD

Tap into the awesome power of meditation, yoga, and a spiritual faith-based perspective to help you maintain a positive expectancy, manage stress, and increase your intuitive, creative powers.

DIVE DEEPER ...

If doubt is dampening your enthusiasm and confidence and faith is something you'd like to cultivate, you'll find strategies to empower yourself throughout my *Career Rescue* series.

Mid-Life Career Rescue-Series Box Set (Books 1-3): The Call For Change, What Makes You Happy, Employ Yourself.

You may like to check out Julia Cameron's book, *Faith and Will,* or find your own sources.

You'll also find free tips and practical strategies on my blog.

YOUR HEALTH IS YOUR WEALTH

30

PROTECT YOUR MENTAL HEALTH

I still have to sit down in peace and write the books.

~ J.K. Rowling

Jessie Burton, author of *The Muse and The Miniaturist*, powerfully sums up how devaluing your health can sneak up on you and the importance of protecting your health—mentally, emotionally, physically, and spirituality.

Below is an extract from the vivid account she shared on her blog earlier in 2017:

"I looked my mental health in the eye and did not do enough to protect it. I burned out again, I suffered dehydration and a viral infection, but far worse, my anxiety came in huge and truly awful doses and, in the end, I had to cancel a few events.

I am well aware of the places I had to cancel events, and one day, I hope to make up for that in those places. It wasn't many, but I did feel terrible.

I truly love having readers, and I did the best I could, a four-month publicity tour, two continents, five events in three days kind of thing, but by the end of September, the scrutiny and analysis, repetition and a sinking of myself led to physical damage and a deep sense of alienation, panic and an indefinable loss.

The thing I want most to do in the world is write, and I agonised that if writing led to this kind of struggle, then what was the solution?" she asked.

Balance. That is the solution. And writing, more than talking about writing," she replied.

It's too late for me to be an Elena Ferrante [an Italian novelist, best known for her *Neapolitan Novels*]. I have thought much about authority, invisibility, how to synthesise the experience of life into fiction in the best ways I can, the ways that feel truest and strongest and will make a reader go with me and say, yes.

A writer's selfhood vies with her need to make herself invisible, in order to freely inhabit a simulacra of multiple lives in fiction (aka Ferrante), and work without worrying about her own received persona in all of it.

A published writer has people pay to read the manifestations of her imagination, soul, and heart.

For me, that remains extraordinary. It will always be the dream transaction for me, but it is also the most exposing, the rawest, unavoidable, supremely important fact in my life that I have battled desperately to understand and get a handle on these past three years.

It's a rockier path, certainly, knowing you are going to be held publicly accountable, knowing that your personhood will be as relevant to your artifices when it comes to talking about the work.

I know I'm not alone in this battle and I am grateful to the other writers who have spoken to me about this on the way, sometimes reaching out without me even having to ask.

"My own lack of anonymity when I publish is something I am coming to accept. I handed it over without even thinking about it.

I made a pact with the kindly devil with my eyes wide shut, but I do not regret it. Having my novels bought and read has been the best thing that ever happened to me.

Sometimes, however, the things that are best for us are not always the easiest. I do regret my inability to find my pause button, but maybe writing that regret here will enable me to locate that mysterious setting inside myself?

I want to write, and write well, and that's nearly all I ever want to do."

Mining for Gold

How can you prepare for inevitable success and avoid overload and overwhelm?

What mental health practices would make a tremendous difference to your sustained prosperity?

You'll find a few helpful reminders and strategies in the chapters which follow.

31

STRESS LESS

Productivity isn't about being a workhorse, keeping busy or burning the midnight oil...It's more about priorities, planning, and fiercely protecting your time.

~ Margarita Tartakovsky, blogger

As Jessie Burton's experience illustrated, when you are under too much pressure, take too much on and don't take time out, you tend to live your life on overdrive and on the verge of burnout.

When you're stressed you are less effective, make more mistakes, suffer more and are prone to illness.

Very often people turn to "medicine"—chemical highs, alcohol, and prescription drugs—to manage the symptoms.

But the reality is that these only offer temporary relief. They mask symptoms which, left unresolved, can set fire to everything you've worked so hard to achieve.

Fortify your resilience. Stop, take a break, rest, eat well, stay away from negative people, cultivate optimism, exercise, do things you love, play, spend time in nature, experience the quietness of solitude, and experiment with other effective stress management techniques.

Mining for Gold

Would you die for success? Destroy your relationships? Sacrifice your mental health?

What can you start, stop, do more or less of to keep your stress levels at a healthy optimum?

Dive deeper...

You'll find more strategies to manage stress and build greater resilience in *Mid-Life Career Rescue: The Call For Change,* and *Stress Less. Love Life More: How to Stop Worrying, Reduce Anxiety, Eliminate Negative Thinking and Find Happiness.*

In the next chapter, we'll look at the many benefits of mindfulness.

32

BE MINDFUL

Our brains never get a break and the results can be increased stress, anxiety, insomnia and, if left unchecked, even depression But there is something you can do—nothing.

~ Mathew Johnstone, author and cartoonist

Many of the most influential authors, creative artists, and business people today credit their meditative practice for their success and prosperity.

"It's the Swiss army knife of medical tools, for conditions both small and large," writes Arianna Huffington, the founder of *The Huffington Post* and author of *Thrive*.

When Tim Ferriss, who practices transcendental meditation, sat down with more than 200 people at the height of their field for his new book, *Tools of Titans*, he found that 80% had some form of guided mindfulness practice.

It took Ferriss a while to get into meditation, he says in a podcast episode about his own morning routine. But since he discovered that the majority of world-class performers meditated, he also decided to follow the habit.

His practice takes up 21 minutes a day: one minute to get settled and 20 minutes to meditate.

Ferriss recommends two apps for those wanting some help getting started—*Headspace* or *Calm*.

"Start small, rig the game so you can win it, get in five sessions before you get too ambitious with length," says Ferriss.

"You have to win those early sessions so you establish it as a habit, so you don't have the cognitive fatigue of that practice."

So, what's the buzz? Here are a few of the many ways a regular meditative practice will improve your mindset:

- Decreased stress and anxiety
- Improved learning ability
- Higher IQ and more efficient brain functioning
- Reduced hyperactivity in the brain, slower wavelengths and decreased beta waves (Beta State:13—30Hz) means more time between thoughts which leads to more skilful decision making
- Increased Theta State (4—8Hz) and Delta States (1—3 Hz) which deepens awareness and strengthens intuition and visualisation skills
- Increased creativity and connection with your higher intelligence

Mining for Gold

Many successful people regularly take time to focus on the present moment. Create space in your day for mindful meditation.

Consistency is key. Shorter meditations on a regular basis are more productive than long sessions every few weeks. If you are a beginner, you may prefer to aim for 5 minutes a day and add 1 minute each week.

Many people find that meditating for 20 minutes in the morning and 20 minutes at the end of the day yields remarkable benefits.

33

SLEEP YOUR WAY TO THE TOP

By helping us keep the world in perspective, sleep gives us a chance to refocus on the essence of who we are. And in that place of connection, it is easier for the fears and concerns of the world to drop away.

~ Arianna Huffington, businesswoman

Time stays long enough for those who use it well and protect it fiercely. But many creatives sacrifice their sleep in the mistaken belief they'll be more productive.

Modern science proves conclusively that if you skip out on sleep, you're compromising not just your creativity and efficiency, but also your health.

"We're suffering a sleep crisis," warns Arianna Huffington, co-founder and editor-in-chief of *The Huffington Post* and author of *The Sleep Revolution: Transforming Your Life One Night at a Time*. The chronic need to be "plugged in" is hurting our health, productivity, relationships, and happiness.

A February 2016 study from the Centres for Disease Control and

Prevention reported that sleeping less than seven hours a day can lead to an increased risk of frequent mental distress, impaired thinking, reduced cognitive ability, and increased susceptibility to depression.

Lack of sleep also increases the likelihood of obesity, diabetes, high blood pressure, heart disease, and stroke. None of which will aid your quest for success.

Try a few of Arianna Huffington's tips to help ensure you get a great sleep:

- Meditate for 20 minutes in the morning and at the end of the day to defrag and reconnect with yourself
- Get ready for bed 30 minutes before bedtime
- Turn off all devices and leave them outside your bedroom
- Only read physical books in bed instead of using an e-reader
- End the day with gratitude—write down three things (or more) you're grateful for
- Have a hot bath with Epsom Salts
- Meditate if you wake in the night

MINING FOR GOLD

Be ruthless about prioritizing your well-being. Remind yourself of the benefits that will flow while you sleep, and sleep more!

34

MOVE INSIDE OUT

*Walking for me is my way of thinking,
my way of meditating.*

~ Paulo Coelho, author

Many writers lead sedentary lives, but the most successful ones praise the benefits of exercise. Many use their exercise as a time to reset and plan.

How much time do you spend outside, communing with nature? Research has shown that most people spend 90 percent of their time indoors, and most of it glued to their laptops, mobile devices, and other technology.

Vitamin D sufficiency, along with diet and exercise, has emerged as one of the most important success factors in human health.

Discipline yourself to go out and get some fresh air—ideally somewhere not too frenzied.

Combine brisk walking with deep breathing to boost your energy levels, short-term memory, and state of mind.

When your breathing is calm and steady, your body is in a nurtured state which helps strengthen your immune system.

Researchers also confirm there is a strong link between breathing, outside energy, and beneficial brainwave patterns. This may explain why so many people say that walking is their meditation—clearing their minds, and allowing space for good ideas to flourish.

"It's not that I am thinking but I am in a kind of trance, totally connected with the present moment," Paulo Coelho says. When he returns to his work, his mind is clear and he is more powerfully connected to source energy.

Mining for Gold

Do you listen to your body barometer when it tells you to exercise more and sloth less?

Monitor how much time you spend indoors. Schedule regular fresh air time, or commit to some type of physical training and movement.

35

MINDFOOD

*If you take care of your mind,
you take care of the world.*

~ Arianna Huffington, businesswoman

Successful people make their health a priority and regularly tune into their body barometers.

It's tougher to succeed if you lack energy, feel stressed, sluggish, lethargic, or unhealthy. Artificially stimulating your mind, body, and soul won't cut it in the long term.

Many of us take for granted how magnificent and clever our bodies are. But for everything to fire optimally, you need to fuel it with food geared for performance, eat mindfully, and not inhale your meal in a race to the finish.

You are what you feed your stomach—which also feeds your mind. For optimum performance, ensure you're putting smart fuel into your body.

Modern nutritionists and health professionals warn of the perils of over and under eating; not eating fresh, seasonal, organic food; and chewing insufficiently.

Diabetes is on the rise. Obesity is an epidemic. Cholesterol and blood pressure are going through the roof. And stress, depression, anxiety, and other mental troubles are all trending upward.

Your gut is also your second brain—a major receptor site of dopamine, a neurotransmitter that helps control the brain's reward and pleasure centres.

Dopamine helps regulate the feel-good emotions we all need to fuel success. It also regulates movement—enabling you to not only see the rewards of your efforts, but to also take action toward them.

Benefits of healthy eating practices include:

- Increased clarity of thinking
- Better memory
- Healthy body weight
- Increased positive emotions
- Enhanced mental, emotional, and physical health
- Improved mood
- More energy and stamina
- Increased goal achievement
- Better sleep
- Longevity

AVOID EXTREMES—TOO much sloth makes one prone to gluttony, too much activity overwhelms, and too many vain pleasures taken to extremes are a cause of failure.

Too much coffee, for example, increases feelings of anxiety. Too much booze, as you'll discover in the next section, can prematurely derail a promising career.

When you switch from eating unhealthily to healthily, the difference will be tangibly transformative.

. . .

MINING FOR GOLD

Try cutting out all sugars, fast foods, high sodium, and processed foods for one week. Limit or cut out coffee and drink 64 ounces of water each day. Journal how you feel to highlight the difference.

Consider booking a check-up with a naturopath or nutritionist. You may be surprised how many allergies are impacting your optimum health.

Research some optimum, high energy foods to nourish your creative brain.

Implement some new healthy eating habits. What can you start, stop, eat more or less of to fuel your success?

36

YOU BOOZE, YOU LOSE

Drinking worked in the beginning: I felt wonderful, warm, and fuzzy...almost pretty...What I didn't know was that I was in a prison of my own making.

~ Colette Baron-Reid, intuitive & author

Alcohol and success don't make good marriage partners, but they're often fatally attracted.

Experience may have already taught you that too much booze muddles the mind, ignites aggression, reduces responsiveness, and ultimately depresses.

It's also hard to quit.

While you don't need to be a teetotaller, alcohol control will make you a better, healthier writer.

Many successful people limit their drinking or consciously decide not to touch a drop. Keeping their resolve often takes extraordinary willpower.

"I spent last weekend suffering from a hangover after too many drinks on Friday night. It literally wiped my weekend and I didn't get any writing done," shares Joanna Penn on one of her blogs.

"I like a glass of wine but I'm not very good on it, and I was very angry with myself for going too far. I have a lot to do at the moment, so I need that time. For me, drinking alcohol does not serve my writing," she said.

Author and public speaker Deepak Chopra gave up drinking. "I liked it too much," he once said. Steven King, after almost losing his family and destroying his writing career, managed to quit.

Julia Cameron, author of *The Artist's Way*, fought her way back from alcoholism. Anne Lamott, author of *Bird by Bird: Some Instructions of Writing and Life*, is a recovered alcoholic.

Other creatives like Amy Winehouse devastatingly never made it. At only 27, she died of alcohol poisoning on July 23, 2011.

Ernest Hemingway committed suicide led from alcoholism, depression, and mental illness. F. Scott Fitzgerald and poet Dylan Thomas also died from poor health related to the complications of alcohol abuse.

Destroying your career, ruining your relationships, sacrificing your sanity, and taking your life is a massive price to pay for your art, or a mistaken belief that to be creative you must drink.

The many benefits of reducing your alcohol intake, or not drinking at all, include:

- A stronger ability to focus on your goals and dreams
- Improved confidence and self-esteem
- Increased productivity
- Increased memory and mental performance
- Better control of your emotions
- Sweeter relationships
- Greater intuition and spiritual intelligence
- Authentic happiness

NOT EVERYONE HAS a battle with booze. Whether you cut back or eliminate alcohol entirely, the choice is ultimately yours. Only you know the benefits alcohol delivers or the success it destroys.

MINING FOR GOLD

Try sobriety. Experiment with living an alcohol-free life.

Consider rejecting or limiting alcohol and replacing it with creativity based on your sober self.

If you'd like to experiment with a period of sobriety or you need help to you moderate your drinking, *Mind Your Drink: The Surprising Joy of Sobriety*, available as a paperback and eBook will help. You can also find a range of books and resources offering help to quit, including alcohol-free alternatives on my website—http://www.cassandragaisford.com/books-and-resources/control-alcohol/

JUST ADD WATER

Water is the driving force in nature.

~ Leonardo da Vinci

As blood is to your heart, so water is to your body. Our bodies are machines, designed to run on water and minerals. Because we're made up of 72 percent of water, it's vitally important for every bodily function.

Insufficient water intake and low consumption of fruit and vegetables can present significant health challenges.

Too much coffee, alcohol, or other diuretics (which increase the amount of water and salt expelled from the body as urine) can also rob your mind and body of energy and vitality.

When you're dehydrated your thoughts become muddled, anxiety can loom, and you'll feel tired, irritable, unmotivated, and generally lacklustre.

In addition to drinking H2O, many prosperous people also find gazing upon or immersing themselves in a body of natural water promotes a positive mindset.

The day before I wrote this chapter, and suffering from a head-cold, I bathed in the hot mineral waters at Ngawha Springs in the far north of New Zealand. Local Maori have long known of the therapeutic properties found by those who bathe in its waters. I felt great, and my energy and health were instantly restored.

It's no coincidence that most millionaires have houses overlooking water.

Mining for Gold

Create more energy and drive by flushing toxins from your body as well as increasing your connection with water. Some simple, but effective, strategies include:

- Drinking at least eight glasses of purified water a day
- Reducing alcohol and coffee
- Consuming more fruits and vegetables—as close to raw as possible
- Splash water on your face whenever you're feeling overwhelmed. Cold water steps up circulation, making you feel invigorated
- Swim in the sea or a lake, or bathe in hot mineral water—either in a natural spring or by adding Epsom Salts (a mineral compound of magnesium and sulphate) to your bath.

38

MAINTAIN SOME BALANCE

Every now and then go away, have a little relaxation, for when you come back to your work your judgment will be surer. Go some distance away because then the work appears smaller and more of it can be taken in at a glance and a lack of harmony and proportion is more readily seen.

~ Leonardo da Vinci

Workaholism is an addiction for many passionate people. Others use overwork to medicate their unhappiness in other areas of their life—most commonly dissatisfaction with their relationships.

When you work slavishly, particularly at something you love, your brain releases chemicals called opiates which create feelings of euphoria. No wonder it's hard to step away!

Euphoria stems from the Greek word *euphoría*—the power of enduring easily. But consider what the state of endurance implies. Enduring implies force or strain, or gritting your teeth and bearing it at times. Force or strain with no respite leads to stress, overload, and burnout—robbing you of vital energy and depleting your millionaire mindset.

Many people find when they don't step away from their work they suffer disillusionment, and things that once filled them with passion, including their current writing project, no longer fills them with joy. Resentment builds and relationships with family, friends, and colleagues can also suffer.

Working addictively offers a short-term fix, but lasting happiness needs variety and nourishment. Being with family or friends, engaging in a hobby, spending time in nature, learning something new, helping others, or just being solitary will help you avoid burnout, nourish your brain, heart, and soul, improve your judgment, and restore harmony.

To be truly happy and successful, you must be able to be at peace when you are working and when you are at rest.

Leonardo da Vinci would often take breaks from his work to refresh his mind and spirit. While others claimed that he took too long to finish things, he knew the importance of replenishing his focus to maintain a clear perspective.

Here we are still talking about him over 500 years later.

Leonardo also valued sleep, noting in one of his journals that some of his best insights came when his mind was not working.

Even if you love the work that you do, and think your book is the greatest thing since man launched into space, it's fun to get away from it and have objective-free time to unwind and reset.

When you return to your work, your focus will be surer, your vision refreshed, and your confidence bolder.

MINING FOR GOLD

Who are you when you are not working? Do you still feel successful? Do you feel worthy?

When was the last time you truly relaxed? Can you think of a time when you stepped away from your work and when you returned, your mind was clearer, your confidence surer?

Schedule time out—and be firm with yourself. Stay away from anything that feeds your addiction.

What can you start doing, stop doing, do more or less of? What benefits will flow from these changes?

39

REAL RESILIENCE

A grit mind strengthens all of your strengths.

~ Pearl Zhu, digital visionary

Ups and downs, highs and lows, troughs and peaks are a rite of passage for many writers.

The fickleness and unpredictability of the publishing world, the extremities of your emotions, the quick and ready insights you experience, the acute sensitivity with which you feel almost everything, can make you vulnerable.

But it doesn't have to be this way. By strengthening your inner power, your ability to handle stressful situations, and your skill in persevering after setbacks threaten to fell you, you'll develop resilient grit.

Grit comes in many shapes and sizes: courage, courageousness, bravery, pluck, mettle, backbone, spirit, steel nerve, resolve, determination, endurance, guts, spunk, tenacity—and the strength of vulnerability. Add the flexibility and determination of resilience and you'll have a winning combination.

Resilience is that indefinable quality that allows some people to be bowled over by life and re-emerge stronger than ever. Rather than letting setbacks overcome them and drain their resolve, they find a way to rise from the ashes.

Psychologists have identified some of the factors that will make you more resilient, among them a positive attitude, optimism, the ability to regulate emotions, and the ability to see failure as a form of helpful feedback.

Life as a writer will keep throwing you curveballs— haters or disenchanted readers may post scathing reviews, your books may not sell in the quantities you hoped, an editor or agent may betray you. Or perhaps life threatens to drown you in a deluge of seemingly never-ending hassles—family dramas, environmental mayhem, world affairs, or some other distraction.

As Buddhists say, life is suffering—it's how you react to a setback that counts. We choose our attitude via our thoughts. "With our thoughts, we make the world," Buddha once said.

Many of the strategies I've shared with you in this book will help you develop a millionaire mindset and with it more staying power, passion, perseverance, and grit.

Mindfulness techniques, avoiding excessive alcohol consumption, keeping your thoughts positive, surrounding yourself with a vibe tribe of positive supporters, getting rid of toxicity (friends, family, or stinkin' thinkin'), meditating, exercise, reprogramming your subconscious beliefs, and other strategies are just some of the things you've learned in *Creating a Millionaire Mindset*.

But, as someone said to me recently, "Life's hard enough without having to do all this 'feel good' stuff." That, dear reader, comes down to choice. Your choice.

Personally, I don't want to live, nor end my life, as F. Scott Fitzgerald did—a poor drunk who felt like a failure and only found success when he was dead.

I don't want to lie in my grave like Amy Winehouse, a dead,

tortured "success" at 27. According to hypnotherapist Marisa Peer, who said Winehouse had cancelled an appointment with her, she had refused to change her mindset. What a sad and tragic waste of talent and potential.

It's not easy to overcome many of the things that hold you back. But you can do it—if you're willing to be strong and fight for your dreams. Within many of us lies an innate seam of strength, which, when mined skilfully, will produce an endless source of pure gold.

As author and filmmaker Michael Moore said, "I want us all to face our fears and stop behaving like our goal in life is merely to survive. Surviving is for game show contestants stranded in the jungle or on a desert island. You are not stranded. Use your power. You deserve better."

I took these words to heart many years ago. Anxiety and depression run in my family—as does a tendency to place a stop-cap on dreams. My grandmother grew up in foster care. Her father murdered a man. I'm sure that her upbringing had an impact on my mom, and in turn, my mom's ability to give me the love I craved as a child.

My dad was dumped in a boarding school when he was only four. He never knew his father, and only found out when he was in his 70s that he had a sister. Growing up, he never experienced a hug or knew true affection.

Like Amy Winehouse and so many others with wounded childhoods, I never felt loved. I've worked hard to overcome the wounds of my childhood.

You should, too. Your past doesn't need to stop you.

"A lot of people feel like they're victims in life, and they'll often point to past events, perhaps growing up with an abusive parent or in a dysfunctional family," writes Rhonda Byrne in *The Secret*.

"Most psychologists believe that about 85 percent of families are dysfunctional, so all of a sudden you're not so unique. My parents were alcoholics. My dad abused me. My mother divorced him when I was six . . . I mean, that's almost everybody's story in some form or not," she says.

Author Jack Canfield also speaks to this point: "The real question is, what are you going to do now? What do you choose now? Because you can either keep focusing on that, or you can focus on what you want. And when people start focusing on what they want, what they don't want falls away, and what they want expands, and the other part disappears."

In hindsight, you will see your life experiences as a gift. As Isabel Allende once said, "Without my unhappy childhood and dysfunctional family, what would I have to write about?"

I channel my life experiences into my books. I pay it forward and share how I learned to empower my mind, body, and soul. I studied Buddhist philosophy. I learned Transcendental and mindfulness meditation.

I devoured nearly every self-help book on the planet—and beyond. I went to healers and sought counselling.

I trained to be a hypnotherapist, counsellor, and psychologist, and gained other therapeutic skills. I continue to pass on the knowledge I've learned to my clients and readers like you to help empower them to live your best lives.

Every day I fight for my dreams.

We all enter this life, and leave it, with different challenges. Different parents, siblings, life experiences. The pain of your past doesn't need to define you. If you are prepared to be honest and vulnerable and to do the work, you know what you need to do to empower your life and your work.

As Buddha once said, "It is better to conquer yourself than to win a thousand battles. Then the victory is yours. It cannot be taken from you, not by angels or by demons, heaven or hell."

Mining for Gold

If fear, wounds of the past, victim thinking, destructive health behaviours, or anything else detrimental to living your best life has a grip on you, prioritise breaking free.

Seeking help doesn't have to cost a fortune. You may heal your life with writing, work with a coach or therapist, or self-help your way to success.

When you seize the reins of control and take responsibility, you will empower your life—and your prosperity.

SLAYING OBSTACLES

40

ALLOW NO DOUBT

Belief without talent will get you further than talent with no belief. If you have the two you will be unstoppable.

~ Marisa Peer, hypnotherapist & author

It's the messages you tell yourself that matter most, according to Marisa Peer.

You may not be aware of your own self-limiting thoughts, beliefs, and patterns, or the negative, confining impact of others' beliefs about you.

Perhaps you've defined your life according to what others think you are capable of or believe you should settle for.

To slay the doubt demons and get at some of the core beliefs standing between you and the success you desire, you must interview your own beliefs.

Ask yourself the following questions:

"Where's your evidence for that?" ("that" being whatever you fear or hold to be true)

"What's the worst that could happen? How bad would that really be?"

"How can you increase the likelihood of success?"

"What tells you that you could follow your dreams?" (a nice shift from focusing on the problem is to look for solutions instead).

"What have you tried recently that worked? What are you doing now that works?"

"Who do you know that is a prosperous author? What could you learn from them?"

"How does your (supportive other) know you can do this? What difference will it make to them when you are happier, prosperous and more successful?"

Affirm What You Want to be True

Your doubts are demons—they will destroy your dreams if you surrender without a fight.

Attitude is everything. Be a guard for your words, thoughts, and feelings. Always affirm what you want to be true and don't let self-doubt be the thing that deflates you.

Winners are too busy to be sad, too positive to be doubtful, too optimistic to be fearful, too focused on success and too determined to be defeated.

Be your biggest fan. Back yourself 100 percent. We all have doubts, but it's amazing how your doubts will disappear once you're doing the things you love.

Mining for Gold

Are you your biggest fan or worst enemy? How can you stay positive, confident, and optimistic?

Be your own CBT (Cognitive Behavioural Therapy) counsellor and continually challenge unhelpful or irrational beliefs.

Empower your beliefs with feeling-based affirmations.

Dive deeper...

You'll find other helpful strategies to boost your beliefs in my book, *Boost Your Self-Esteem and Confidence: Six Easy Steps to Increase Self-Confidence, Self-esteem, Self-Value and Love Yourself More.*

I've also included a helpful section in my book, *Mid-Life Career Rescue: What Makes You Happy.* In this book, I share my experience following reading The Biology of Belief: Unleashing the Power of Consciousness, Matter & Miracles, by Dr. Bruce Lipton.

The chapters which follow will help keep doubt low and confidence high.

41

FINANCE YOUR WRITING CAREER

You may not have the cash at the moment, and the economy may not be ideal, but that doesn't mean your mind can't be working on your ideas and creating the way to a better future. Look for opportunities in every climate. That's leverage.

~ Cassandra Gaisford

Many people dream of writing a book or making a living from their writing but say that lack of spare cash is holding them back. They prevent themselves from choosing what they want to do because they fear there won't be the necessary money or support to allow it.

But money doesn't have to be an obstacle to seeking more fulfilling work. Financing a career change, despite all the obstacles in your way, involves a conscious commitment to move forward and a willingness to think laterally and pragmatically about a range of financial options.

There are many different ways to finance a career change, including: consolidating debt, future-gazing and demand creation, career combo-ing, seeking investors, using equity, reducing outgoings, generating extra cash flow, and applying for funding.

The discipline needed to reprioritise your finances will be easier, and the sacrifices more bearable, if you allow your desire to drive you. Let's take a closer look at some of the possible financing options:

Rewrite your goals. List all the benefits making a change will bring. These may include better health, more money in the longer term, or improved relationships with loved ones.

Assess your current situation. Get an accurate picture of all your outgoings and expenses. Consolidate debt. Seek financial advice if necessary.

Get a reality check on your future plans. Is there a current or future demand for your writing? Could you create one? What is the true cost of making a change? Isolate costs against benefits: cash in against cash out. How much money do you really need to spend and create?

Earn more. Think laterally to create cash flow. A job doesn't have to be a full-time thing. Can you finance your career by doing a career-combo, working in a variety of different ways, or for several employers? Many people work at several jobs to earn extra cash.

Generate extra cash flow by increasing the money you earn. Some possible strategies include: negotiating a pay rise in your current position; taking on a new higher-paying role; or turning a hobby into cash flow.

New Zealand based and *USA Today* bestselling historical romance author Bronwen Evans, for example, took on a high-paying, high-pressure, one-year communications contract to allow her to take a year off so she could pursue her dream of becoming a full-time novelist.

Seek investors. Use other people's money to create the momentum you need. Remember there's good borrowing—borrowing to increase wealth, and bad borrowing—borrowing so you can consume more. Most people spend all their spare income on non-asset-producing consumption.

Banks, family members, and friends are all possible sources of investment income. Sam Morgan, who established the on-line trading company TradeMe, convinced his dad to back him and earned millions of dollars in return. You may not pay back millions, but if your idea is sound, your investors can sleep at night knowing they will be repaid.

Utilise equity. Burt Munro, whose story was made famous in the movie *The World's Fastest Indian*, mortgaged his home. Could you use the equity in your own home to finance your career? If you don't want to re-mortgage, you could try asking for a mortgage holiday. Many banks allow 2–3 months of no mortgage payments.
As fashion designer Calvin Klein once said, "I took the risk of putting my money on the line for the company." Are you prepared to do the same thing?

Share the load. Who else has a stake in your success? Perhaps they may be able to inject more cash into your joint cash flow or pitch in and share the family load.
New Zealand romance author Leanna Morgan asked her husband to take on the day-to-day family commitments so she could focus on her writing.

Today, she's a *USA Today* bestselling author who sells up to 300 books a day and has legions of fans in America. She's also the CEO of her own publishing company.
In just two years, Morgan has gone from an unknown writer to one who earns over $200,000 a year, allowing the mother-of-two to give

up her job as a Libraries and Arts Manager to concentrate on her writing.

She recently shared with me that her goal is to make a million dollars, and more, from her writing.

"If anyone had told me two years ago that I'd be able to resign from a job I loved to become a full-time writer and publisher, I would have smiled and thought they were slightly crazy. But believe it or not, that's what happened," she told journalist Anna Kenna.

"Her success has not been without sacrifice, including little sleep and less time with husband Tim and her two children, aged 12 and 17," Kenna writes in her article.
"'I'd be up at 5.30am, getting in a few hours of writing before work, and writing in the evening when everybody else was asleep.'"

So she could devote herself to writing, Leanna's husband Tim shared more of their responsibilities.

"'Tim took over running the house and organising our children,'" Morgan says. "'He did it to support me, but also because he could see the potential benefits of my success for the whole family.'"

Sharing the load, hard work, and commitment have yielded success beyond her and her family's dreams.

"'It's taken away the financial stress, allowed us to take a nice holiday and to look forward to a future we never considered possible,'" she says.

Find out more about Leanna Morgan at www.leeannamorgan.com and read the rest of this article, including why it's a brilliant time to be an independent author, here: www.stuff.co.nz/entertainment/books/85799137/How-one-Kiwiauthor-is-making-200-000-a-year-publishing-romance-novels-online.

Reduce outgoings. Review your current commitments and expenditure. Proactively look around to make sure you are getting the best deal possible on your insurance, mobile phone plans, mortgages, and other regular financial commitments. Take note of your savings and squirrel the extra money away for a rainy day.

John, a coaching client of mine, shopped around for a better deal on his household insurance and saved himself over $600 annually in premiums. He also negotiated an instalment plan with creditors so that he could increase his credit debt repayments, saving over $5,400 in interest charges annually.

Get funded. Many people and organisations offer sponsorship and various forms of funding to help people pursue their dreams. Without the help of a grant from Creative New Zealand, author Lloyd Jones may never have written *Mr. Pip*—the same book for which he won the prestigious and lucrative Man Booker Prize. The book was later made into a film.

Check out crowdfunding as an option, as Heather Morris initially shared in the chapter "Knock the Bugger Off." Her attempts to finance her film script lead to a multi-national publishing deal.

Multiply your income streams. When "authorpreneur" Kevin Kruse made the move to self-employment, he decided to record his financial success, complete with the highs and lows, by publicly sharing his income reports on his blog. There's lots of inspiration for anyone about to embrace change here: http://authorjourneyto100k.com/income-report-december-2015-and-full-year/.

Like many business people, Kruse knew early on that having a variety of income streams would help him manage cash-flow.

"I went into this whole thing knowing that to make the money I wanted to make I would need to diversify my income. I knew I'd need to spend time speaking, creating online courses, and marketing."

It is a common and successful strategy used by many business people, especially those working creatively. Ruth Pretty, for example, is a chef, newspaper columnist, cookbook writer, wedding venue provider, caterer, and cooking school tutor. The common theme? Her pursuits all centre around her passion for food.

Amongst other things, photographer Carla Coulson is a portrait photographer, magazine photojournalist, tutor, and travel photographer. At the time of writing, she has retrained as a life coach and now offers creativity coaching and wellness workshops.

Italian designer Giorgio Armani has a flourishing clothing empire, a swag of luxury hotels, a music production company, and an interior design business. And these are just a few of his multi-billion-dollar revenue lines.

I am a self-empowerment author, coach, romance writer, brand manager, and novelist of art-related historical fiction. I also write marketing materials (blogs, newsletters, website content, etc.) for small businesses, and train people to become certified life and career coaches.

As my writing income grows, I'm making a conscious decision to spend less time in some of these areas and more in others.

You may wish to focus on one income stream, but if this doesn't work for you, consider diversifying. This will help you ride any fluctuating financial currents.

Remind yourself that money is not a measure of your true worth.

Clarify what's important to you. As business magnate Richard Branson said, "I don't work for money, that's too shallow a goal." Lucky for him, his passion for having fun has netted him millions—as it has for James Patterson and other prosperous authors.

Whatever path you choose, be sure to work with love. Sonia Choquette, author of *Your Heart's Desire*, echoes this view: "When you work with love you draw others to you. Embrace this truth. The reason for this is that love is the highest vibration on earth. When you work with love people feel it, are helped by it, and return to it. That's why love is the best marketing tool around. Because it is so attractive, it pulls right to you what you need."

The Money or Your Life

His Holiness the Dalai Lama once said, "Choose a job that allows the opportunity for some creativity and for spending time with your family. Even if it means less pay—it is better to choose work that is less demanding, that gives you greater freedom, more time to be with your family and friends, engage in cultural activities or just play. I think that is best."

This really spoke to me and was one of the primary reasons I chose to scale back my successful international consultancy. Time is more valuable to me than money. I can always find ways to get more money, but it is impossible to find more than 24 hours in any one day.

Be careful what you chase. Is it more money, or a better quality of life? With planning, it just may be possible to do both, says Tim Ferris in his bestselling book *The 4-Hour Work Week*.

Mining for Gold

How could you finance your writing career?

42

FIGHT FOR YOUR DREAMS

Remember your dreams and fight for them. You must know what you want from life. There is just one thing that makes dreams become impossible: the fear of failure.

~ Paulo Coelho, author

Novelist Steven Pressfield called it as it is when he titled his non-fiction book *The War of Art*.

It's war out there with many opponents—time, temptation, distraction, economic uncertainty, family, work demands, and more.

Very often you may find that you are your own worst enemy and are either consciously or unconsciously sabotaging your success.

As Jessie Burton, a successful novelist who suffers from anxiety once said, "If you really want to see your work to completion you have to desire it more than you believe. You have to fight it, fight yourself. It's not easy."

To help overcome some of the many things impeding your dreams, you must strive to acquire the following mindsets:

1.) **A willingness to persevere.** Many authors' first novels, and their subsequent ones, even when they were at the height of their fame, were rejected.

"Perseverance is absolutely essential, not just to produce all those words, but to survive rejection and criticism," J.K. Rowling once wrote.

2.) **An ability to handle criticism—even laugh at it.** At a writer's conference I attended several years ago, Micheal Cunningham, the Pulitzer Prize-winning author of *The Hours*, was told by a man, "I loved your first book but I hate this one. I really think you've lost it."

I was shocked and the audience was aghast. After taking a moment to compose himself, Michael, who is openly gay, smiled and said, "I'm sorry if we have to break up over this honey. I write the books I want to read. If you like it great. If not, that's fine too."

The audience laughed and Michael's light-hearted and humorous response only added to his appeal.

3.) **An ability to fear less.** Many authors are self-critical about their abilities. Some feel anxiety, others despondency. Elizabeth Gilbert, author of *Eat, Pray, Love*, once shared how she feared she would never write another #1 bestselling book. But she showed up and wrote more books any way.

She's used this same courage to announce that she is now in a same-sex relationship with a woman who was diagnosed with cancer.

"Death—or the prospect of death—has a way of clearing away everything that is not real," she said. "In that space of stark and utter realness, I was faced with this truth: I do not merely love Rayya; I am in love with Rayya. And I have no more time for denying that truth."

In the end, what matters is being true to yourself and cherishing the dreams which feel most real.

"I stopped pretending to myself that I was anything other than what I was, and began to direct all my energy into finishing the only work that mattered to me," J.K. Rowling once said.

How skilfully are you fighting for your dream of becoming a prosperous author?

Other than finishing and applying the strategies in this book, what additional tools, support, or weapons could help you fight through the blocks and win your inner creative battles?

How can you stay true to your vision and keep everything real?

43

SHIFTING SELF-LIMITING BELIEFS

I told my audience that if they changed their beliefs they could change their lives. It was a familiar conclusion with familiar responses from participants: 'Well Bruce, that's great, but how do we do that?'

~ Bruce Lipton, developmental biologist

So often, we aren't even aware of what our self-limiting beliefs are. If your unhelpful thoughts are ingrained, or you keep sabotaging your own success, seeking help from a qualified practitioner with expertise in reprogramming stubborn, disempowering beliefs may be a game-changer.

A wonderful counsellor with whom I trained to be a Worklife Solutions Certified Life Coach recommended the book *The Biology of Belief: Unleashing the Power of Consciousness, Matter & Miracles*, by Bruce Lipton.

Lipton is an American developmental biologist best known for promoting the idea that genes and DNA can be manipulated by a person's beliefs.

In his book, he shares how he experienced a paradigm shift while at a conference. Back then, Lipton, like so many of us, didn't fully realise the crucial role the subconscious mind plays in the change process.

"Instead, I relied mostly on trying to power through negative behaviour, using positive thinking and willpower. I knew, though, that I had had only limited success in making personal changes in my own life.

"I also knew that when I offered this solution, the energy in the room dropped like a lead balloon. It seems my sophisticated audiences had already tried willpower and positive thinking with limited success."

Fate intervened for Lipton, as it did for me when I was guided to his book. So often life whispers to us, but we fail to tune in. In Lipton's case, the messenger he needed to hear was sitting right next to him; psychotherapist Rob Williams, the creator of the self-help tool PSYCH-K, was presenting at the same conference.

"Rob's opening remarks quickly had the entire audience on the edge of our seats. In his introduction, Rob stated that PSYCH-K can change long-standing, limiting beliefs in a matter of minutes," Lipton wrote.

In his book *The Biology of Belief*, Lipton shares how, in less than 10 minutes, a woman paralysed by her fear of public speaking transformed into a confident, excited, and visibly relaxed person up on the stage. The transformation Lipton witnessed was so astounding, he has since used PYSCH-K in his own life.

"PSYCH-K has helped me undo my self-limiting beliefs, including one about not being able to finish my book," Lipton wrote at the end of his book.

That struck a chord with me. I felt a trill of excitement. Not a thrill, but a trill—a song deep in my heart. Lipton was like the Pied Piper and I was happy to follow. At the time, I had so many unfinished books and had published nothing.

A month after working with a PSYCH-K trained practitioner, I finished the first two books in my *Mid-Life Career Rescue* series. Soon after, I released my third, *Midlife Career Rescue: Employ Yourself*, followed quickly by a fourth book, *How to Find Your Passion and Purpose*.

At the time of writing, I have also published three romance books under my pen name, Mollie Mathews.

Now, you're reading my twelfth book—all completed within the last two years. All because, despite feeling skeptical (and a little vulnerable), I sought help to reprogram my mindset.

Mining for Gold

If your unhelpful beliefs are ingrained, or you keep sabotaging your own success, seeking help from a qualified practitioner with expertise in reprogramming stubborn, disempowering beliefs may be a game-changer.

Chances are you don't need to see a therapist to move beyond self-limiting beliefs; but if you do, go and get help. There's magic in that.

You can also learn from some of the most powerful, effective, and simple techniques used by practitioners working in the realm of positive psychology and mind reprogramming. This includes hypnosis—something you'll discover in the next chapter.

44

HYPNOTIZE YOUR MILLIONAIRE MIND

Hypnosis is the epitome of mind-body medicine. It can enable the mind to tell the body how to react and modify the messages that the body sends to the mind.

~ New York Times

To get the tremendous power of your unconscious mind behind your goals, you will need to program it for success. A simple and exceedingly effective way to do this is through hypnosis.

"Emotional problems work much more on the 'feeling level' than the 'thinking level' which is why just trying to think differently is so hard," say the UK-based hypnotherapists at Uncommon Knowledge. "We use hypnosis to help you feel different quickly which then makes you think differently about a situation."

You'll recall in the chapter "What Do You Believe?" that we discussed how important reprogramming your thinking and feeling world is to your success. You can access hypnosis sessions from the comfort of your home via instant download. But a word of caution first—the Internet is awash with websites which offer hypnosis products and services that have not been created by experienced and qualified professionals. Some of these programs are of limited or no use, while others may do more harm than good.

One of my favourite hypnosis sites is run by the UK-based company Uncommon Knowledge. On their website, www.hypnosisdownloads.com, you'll find a range of self-hypnosis mp3 audios, including *The Millionaire Mindset* program. In their own words, they confirm that the program contains the following six success-shaping sessions:

1) Create Winning Business Ideas—enter a creative space within your mind where the money-making ideas will flow like molten gold.

2) Create Real Business Passion—generate a powerful deep unconscious drive for your business idea that will propel you forward.

3) Build Unshakeable Self-Belief—every successful entrepreneur has solid self-confidence and self-belief. Build yours so you can beat the nay-sayers and weather the storms with ease.

4) Generate Laser Focus—you don't get to the top by drifting off and thinking about other things. Get the full power of your unconscious mind behind your goals.

5) Develop an Unstoppable Work Ethic—anyone who tells you becoming a millionaire is not hard work has never done it. This session will make work your most enjoyable pastime.

6) Create Unbeatable Optimism—as you travel your business path, you will come up against obstacles. There will be times when you wonder if you should give up. This session will give you a solid bedrock of optimism, so you just know it's going to work, even on the darkest of days.

Mining for Gold

Research the benefits of hypnosis and experiment with this powerful technique.

45

JUST DO IT

The only thing that makes me feel good about writing is making progress.

~ Aaron Sorkin, screenwriter

It's hard to make a living from your writing if you're not actually writing. This is obvious. Yet it's amazing how compelling the refrigerator can seem, or how exciting cleaning your house can appear, or going to fetch groceries—anything to avoid sitting down at the keyboard and writing.

Some people call this resistance; others say they are simply blocked. For many writers, this state of inertia before they get into the energy of their project is commonplace.

Oscar-winning screenwriter Aaron Sorkin once said, "People ask me if I ever get writer's block and I have to laugh—because that is my default position. I am in a constant state of writer's block. Somehow or other you spring yourself from jail."

Your get out of jail card may be as simple as declaring war and placing 10 words on the page, committing to 15 minutes of writing, or giving yourself permission to write crap.

Aaron Sorkin says when he is feeling really blocked, he'll jump in his car, wind up the sounds, and drive until the ideas flow again.

Paulo Coelho goes for a walk and gives himself a sound talking to. Nora Roberts stops making excuses and writes to avoid feeling guilty.

I find that maintaining a daily habit of writing first thing in the morning, and setting the timer for 15-minute sprints if I'm feeling blocked or sluggish, works for me.

Once you're back in the energy of your book or writing project, you'll find it easy to keep making progress. Whatever it takes to get going again, the most important thing is that you will have won a victory over yourself. You will have conquered writer's block.

MINING FOR GOLD

List your winning strategies to conquer resistance, writer's block, or whatever is hindering you from "just doing it."

What could you start doing, stop doing, do more of, or less of to win the war of art?

46

TAKE THE PROCRASTINATION CHALLENGE

I hold Olympic records for procrastination. I can procrastinate thinking about my procrastination problem. I can procrastinate dealing with my problem of procrastinating thinking about my procrastination problem.

~ Robert McKee, story doctor

It might seem counterproductive, but sometimes the best way to get into the right mindset is radical acceptance—flow with your current mindset.

"It's how I am," Paulo Coelho told Tim Ferris about his daily battle with procrastination. "I don't have deadlines. I write a book once every two years. I sit down of course, I have the book inside me.

"I start procrastinating in the morning. I check my emails, I check news—I check anything that I could check just to avoid the moment to sit and face myself as a writer in front of my book.

"For three hours, I am trying to tell myself, 'No, no, no. Later, later, later.' Then later, not to lose face in front of myself, I tell myself to sit and write for half an hour. And of course, this half an hour becomes 10 hours in a row.

"That's why I write my books so quickly. Very quickly, because I cannot stop. And then of course at night I take a lot of notes because I am still in the speed of writing the book, the next day these notes are useless.

"The same thing happens again: checking emails, going to social communities, postponing, procrastinating. And this I cannot stop; it's my ritual. I have to feel guilty for not writing for three hours or four hours. But then I start writing non-stop. In two weeks, I have the book ready.

"But, my daily schedule of writing is as I just described: trying to escape from my books."

Coelho is not alone.

"I've been a published author since 1974, writing several books every year since—188 now with 21 *New York Times* bestsellers and 70 million copies sold. For decades, I've also been teaching writing and how to get published, all the while facing every excuse and objection imaginable," says millionaire-author and writing teacher Jerry Jenkins.

"'It's easier for you,'" students in his classes tell him. "'Because you're well-known, you write faster than I do, you're obviously more disciplined then I am, you can't be a procrastinator like I am.'"

"When I tell them they're talking to the king of procrastinators, their looks alone call me a liar," Jenkins says. "It's time to put on your big kid pants and face the truth," he tells his students. "If you want it badly enough, you can do what I do." We'll dive deeper into some of Jenkins' strategies in the next chapter.

Mining for Gold

How can you slay the procrastination dragon?

Intensify your desire. Revisit, "Cultivate a Burning Desire."

KEEP YOUR DEADLINES SACRED

Keep your deadline sacred—even if it's self, rather than publisher, imposed. No matter how long you delay, stall, procrastinate, and increase the number of pages per day you must write to make your deadline, there absolutely has to be a limit.

~ Jerry Jenkins, author

"It's true—I am a procrastinator. In fact, I'm the worst. And it once paralysed me," admits Jerry Jenkins.

It's affirming to know that many of the most successful authors face the same daily obstacles as newbies who are starting their writing careers.

Rather than admit defeat, established authors roll up their sleeves, stretch their writing fingers, and power-up their millionaire mindset with strategies they know work.

"Believe me, I've seen this monster try to morph into writer's block, that most terrifying of all boogeymen," says Jenkins.

"How bad was I? I should ask, how bad *am* I? Because the truth is,

I have not rid myself of the curse. I have merely learned how to manage it. And you can, too.

"I try everything to keep from falling further and further behind. I change locations, eliminate distractions, and still find myself stalling, delaying, changing those numbers of pages per day on my calendar, committed to make my deadline.

"But before I found the answer, I had trouble sleeping, despite my dogged determination to really, finally get started the next day.

"Naturally, that led to only more frustration. For even if I somehow found the spark—or whatever I needed—I would be too exhausted to write.

"As a person of faith, of course I had been praying throughout the ordeal—every time, all the time. So, it shouldn't have surprised me that an answer came. To my shame, I didn't immediately recognise it as divine cause and effect. As I too often do, I merely accepted it as my good fortune."

Jenkins had been procrastinating— by researching procrastination— and says that by chance he stumbled upon something useful and freeing. "The secret to overcoming procrastination," he says, "is don't stop procrastinating.

"You read that right. Don't try to beat it or avoid it. Rather, expect it, plan for it, schedule it. And believe—know—that while you're procrastinating, your subconscious is working on your book. Then you'll be able to rest, even to sleep."

The #1 Requirement that Ensures Your Success

Jenkins says his master strategy is to keep your deadline sacred—even if it's self, rather than publisher-imposed. "No matter how long you delay, stall, procrastinate, and increase the number of pages per day you must write to make your deadline, there absolutely has to be a limit. You cannot let things get to the point where there are too many pages per day for you to write. Trust me, that's how you can learn to live at peace with procrastination."

Jenkins says, "Now, when I have a deadline, I:

1.) Dutifully schedule my daily writing plan

2.) Know full well I'll stall and delay and go through my ridiculous rituals, unable to get started when I know I should

3.) Relax and sleep well anyway, knowing my subconscious is working on my book

4.) Keep a careful eye on the calendar so I don't let the days get out of hand

5.) Keep my deadline sacred

6.) Finally, start when I really have to and enjoy discovering the surprises my subconscious reveals."

Author Isabel Allende holds to a very strict writing routine to slay procrastination. She takes herself off to a dedicated writing room and writes on a computer, working Monday through Saturday, 9:00 A.M. to 7:00 P.M.

She also has a sacred day on which she always begins her books. "I always start on January 8," she once said. This is a tradition she began in 1981 with the letter she wrote to her dying grandfather that would become *The House of the Spirits*.

Mining for Gold

Take a page from Jerry Jenkins' phenomenal success. Work with procrastination and schedule it into your day.

Create a daily writing plan.

Create your own deadlines and keep these sacred.

48
FOCUS

The mind that engages in subjects of too great variety becomes confused and weakened.

~ Leonardo da Vinci

There are divergent thoughts on what it means to be focused. Some people believe you should focus on only one thing, one task, one priority, one book at a time.

Only when you have finished that task do you move to the next. Great! If that works for you, you have your success strategy.

But some people thrive on variety. Seeing one thing through to the end often bores them—stifling their creativity and productivity.

If a lack of focus is something getting in your way, really drill down into the causal factors. Play the role of scientist. Discover the cause, identify the effect, hypothesise solutions, and experiment until you find a strategy that works. Perhaps the issue is less about focus and more about self-discipline!

Eckhart Tole, author of *The Power of Now*, advocates surrender.

Whatever is holding your attention now—surrender to it. Focus on what you 'should' be doing at a later date.

Juggling too many balls? Prioritise them, set a timer, and allocate segmented time for all the competing activities you feel must get done.

Practice creative procrastination. Ask yourself, "What is the best use of my time right now?" Put off everything else.

Gary Keller, in his bestselling book *The One Thing*, advocates going small—narrow your concentration at any one time to one thing. Ask yourself, "What's the ONE thing you can do this week (or whatever time period works for you) such that by doing it everything else would be easier or unnecessary?"

You may find that too much environmental mayhem is hindering your prosperous mindset. Studies have shown that a cluttered environment restricts your ability to focus. Consider streamlining your environment to create the ultimate mindset.

Mining for Gold

Remind yourself of a time when you struggled to focus. What worked then that you could apply now?

Focus your energy on the things that are important to you. What is the ONE thing you can do this week which will make doing everything else easier or unnecessary?

Declutter your environment.

49

CONSULT THE ORACLES

Faith in the guidance of Spirit gives you the courage to take risks, because you're assured that whatever happens, a Higher Power is on your side and you will survive.

~ Colette Baron-Reid, intuitive & author

Subjects such as astrology, psychic phenomena, spirituality, and a fascination with tarot and oracle cards have helped many creative people and successful entrepreneurs overcome doubt, strengthen their beliefs, clarify their direction and find meaning in challenging situations.

As I share in my book *The Art of Success: How Extraordinary Artists Can Help You Succeed in Business and Life*, Coco Chanel, like many people, found great wisdom, peace, comfort, and healing from oracle cards and an eclectic array of spiritual rituals.

It is also believed that one of the cards in Coco's *Lenormand* deck inspired one of the secret ingredients contained in Chanel N°5.

My first experience with psychic phenomena and the Tarot was when I was a teenager in New Zealand in the late 70s. Like Coco, it's a fascination that stayed with me throughout my life and which continues to provide inspiration, courage, and fortitude—both personally and professionally.

My daughter is also a gifted intuitive and offers angel card readings professionally via her business Co-Creators of Joy.

"Increasing numbers of people are looking to ancient oracles to receive personal guidance because they are not getting the answers and insights they need when they consult the usual sources of psychology and science," says intuitive counsellor Colette Baron-Reid.

However, there are some highly influential psychologists who honour the wisdom and intuitive guidance that oracles herald.

Of all the psychological theories in the West, that of revered Swiss psychologist Carl Jung stands out as most applicable to Tarot.

Jung wrote about Tarot on several occasions, seeing it as depicting archetypes of transformation like those he found in myths, dreams, and alchemy.

He described its divinatory abilities as similar to the ancient divination text I Ching and to astrology, and later in life established a group which attempted to integrate insights about a person based on multiple divination systems including Tarot.

APPLYING Oracles to Your Writing Day

As Colette Baron-Reid writes in the foreword to her newest Tarot deck *The Good Tarot*, "This version of the tarot is all about goodness, birthing our awareness of our true selves, and expressing that in our lives.

"It's about happiness, compassion, love, and finding our faith and living it regardless of temporary outer conditions."

At the time of writing this chapter, I felt a little discouraged by some personal challenges. I drew a card at random from *The Good Tarot*. The card I drew was "2 of Fire." I smiled when I saw the image on the front of the card—a girl sitting astride a beautiful golden giraffe.

I love giraffes. Blue Giraffe Publishing, the company I founded for my self-empowerment books, is of course inspired by these gracious creatures with their huge hearts.

Instantly I felt a surge of joyful connection. The message which Colette provides in the accompanying guidebook is provided below —I'm sure it will have relevance for you:

2 of Fire

Creative planning for the future, mapping progress, trusting in the unknown, Spirit inspired ambition.

Whenever I can't see how my dreams will coalesce into form, I can trust in the process of co-creation and engage more deeply in the process of envisioning something new.

I have already started to make progress, and soon my passion will attract the perfect situation for me. The light go Spirit helps me to see my way and feel the Universe and aligning to bring me what I need.

This card reminded me that even when I can't see the results of my intentions, I must continue to trust Spirit and the magnetism of writing and creating with passion.

As Dame Anita Roddick, founder of the organic skincare company The Body Shop once said, "We create with passion and passion sells."

The lantern on the oracle card which dangles from the giraffe's mouth also reminds of the message I share in the chapter "Chase the Light."

"Although its messages are about positivity and how to find meaning and attain a positive result no matter what the flow of results," says Colette Baron in her introduction, "*The Good Tarot* doesn't shy away from the truth of our sufferings.

"Instead, it gives us hope that no matter how many times we stumble, we nevertheless find immense treasures as we discover our true natures as spiritual beings expressing ourselves through the art of living in the realm of form."

I notice oracles everywhere. You will, too, when you tune your mindset to listen to the wisdom that surrounds you.

As I write this chapter at my favourite café, a song with the lyrics "I won't stay in a world without love" is playing. There is a love heart infused within the froth of my coffee.

And these signs, combined with the giraffe on the tarot card, all reaffirm to me the importance of writing with passion and sending love letters to the world to help and encourage other authors like you.

Not everyone believes in mysticism—and that's fine. But I do. And so do a great many people.

"If you want to be a serious writer or intellectual you can't say you're a mystic because no one will talk to you again," says American author (and professional tarot card reader) Jessa Crispin, slightly tongue-in-cheek.

Crispin, Colette Barron-Reid, and other creative people like myself are proud to join many others who invite people to experience a new, or rather old way, of living an inspired life.

Mining for Gold

Experiment with tarot—either have a reading with an experienced tarot card reader or study the cards and their meanings for yourself.

Feed your curiosity—take note of the places and circumstances where tarot, astrological symbols, and other mystical and occultist philosophies are used—in business and life.

50
JOURNAL YOUR WAY TO SUCCESS

I love my writing journal. It's my partner in writing, there for me whenever I need it, my confidant and my supporter and my record of where I've been.

~ Anne Gracie, romance author

Recently, while tackling a mammoth writing project, I talked myself into a bit of a funk. I knew that what I really needed was some positive reminders of my intentions. Instead of saying "I quit" and "I am so over this," and retelling the story that allowed for failure, I went online and purchased a beautiful black sketchbook.

Prior to this, I had noticed anxiety building—as it always does when I don't have a special book in which to purge and reshape my thoughts.

With my gold pen, I wrote some of the most empowering and encouraging quotes from other authors who have also struggled to maintain a prosperous mindset while writing an epic book.

Top of my list was Jessie Burton's empowering words, "Always picture succeeding, never let it let it fade. Always picture success, no matter how badly things seem to be going in the moment."

These words reminded me that I was picturing failure. I was telling myself messages of failure. I was feeling failure.

Jesse Burton, the author of *The Muse and The Miniaturist*, is very inspiring to me because she is so honest about her own battles with mental health—including anxiety.

"In February, I was publicly honest about how difficult it had been to handle, process and assimilate in real time some of the changes in my life. Namely, the strange and wondrous effects of *The Miniaturist*. I wrote about anxiety, my first tentative foray into putting that mental morass into words," she wrote in one of her newsletters.

As Burton highlights, blogging and sharing your thoughts with your fans is another form of cathartic journaling—as is writing a book like this.

"You could have talked more about your personal experience so that other writers can more easily relate to you," wrote an advance reader of this book.

You'll notice in this chapter and throughout this book that I've woven in more of my experiences, the highs and the lows, as a result.

To boost your success mindset, another form of journaling is writing Morning Pages, a strategy developed by Julia Cameron, author of *The Artist's Way*.

The writing is just a stream of consciousness, writing out whatever you are feeling—good (or what one of my clients calls the "sunnies") or not so good ("the uglies").

"It's a way of clearing the mind—a farewell to what has been and a hello to what will be," Cameron says.

"Write down just what is crossing your consciousness. Cloud thoughts that move across consciousness. Meeting your shadow and taking it out for a cup of coffee so it doesn't eddy your consciousness during the day."

The point of this writing is to work with your subconscious and let it work its magic in the creative, healing process.

. . .

Mining for Gold

Keep a writing journal for specific writing projects. It may not work for you, but you will never know until you try.

Start where you are—commit to a daily practice of writing Morning Pages and journal for self-exploration.

Dive Deeper...

You can find out more about Morning Pages here http://juliacameronlive.com/basic-tools/morning-pages/

51

MAKE MISTAKES

And then, out of many years of silence and failure and feeling that my whole life was a disaster, the writer came, like a blessing, like a door that opened into another space.

~ Isabel Allende

Conquering failure often requires learning the hard way to reach dizzying heights and allowing room for disappointment.

One successful author, whose name escapes me, once advised aspiring authors to affirm the following, "I am willing to write badly; I am willing to do the work whether it is any good or not; I am also willing to allow brilliance."

Many people stagnate under the weight of perfectionism or fear of failing because they worry about making mistakes.

It may be challenging, but investing in strategies to create more tolerance and acceptance towards making mistakes will prove liberating. One strategy is to learn from others' misfortune.

With hindsight, sometimes the greatest fortune comes from

making the biggest blunders. Here are just a few mistakes that turned out well:

Isabel Allende started her career in journalism and soon found herself offside with people who didn't appreciate her outspoken views. For years she felt under-appreciated—until she decided to tackle her first novel, *The House of Spirits*.

The novel was named Best Novel of the Year in Chile in 1982, and Allende received the country's Panorama Literario award. *The House of the Spirits* has been translated into over 37 languages. It was also adapted into a film of the same name starring Jeremy Irons, Meryl Streep, Winona Ryder, Glenn Close, and Antonio Banderas.

Musician Ornette Coleman's mistake led her to be acclaimed as the inventor of "free jazz." She was awarded the MacArthur Fellowship (nicknamed the Genius Award) in 1994 and the Pulitzer Prize for Music in 2007.

"It was when I found out I could make mistakes that I knew I was on to something," she once said.

Walt Disney was fired by a newspaper for lack of ideas. He also went bankrupt several times before he and his brother co-founded Walt Disney Productions, one of the best-known motion picture production companies in the world. Disney's revenue last year was $US45 billion.

Dr. Suess' first children's book, *And to Think That I Saw it on Mulberry Street*, was rejected by 27 publishers. The 28th publisher, Vanguard Press, sold six million copies of the book. He went on to write numerous other books which still sell well today.

Rhonda Byrne's life was at an all-time low. Fifty-five and twice divorced, her father had just died and her career was in crisis.

That was until, acting on an inspired thought, she created the DVD *The Secret* and later produced a book, both of which galloped away to become some of the biggest-selling self-help resources of all time.

At the heart of Byrnes' inspirational series of products is the Law of Attraction.

"Everything in your life is attracted to you by what you are thinking," Rhonda says. "You are like a human transmission tower, transmitting a frequency with your thoughts. If you want to change anything in your life, change the frequency by changing your thoughts."

Refuse to be a victim. Next time you feel you've made a mistake, ask yourself, "How could this work out for my highest good?"

Be gentle with yourself. Sometimes making mistakes heralds a time of new birth and energy. Draw on the lessons you have learned to help you move forward.

Notice how you have grown and changed as a result of everything that has happened. Gather information as you go and be ready for a new adventure. Look for positive signs for successful outcomes in the future.

Mining for Gold

What is the biggest mistake you ever made and what did you learn?

Buoy your resolve by collecting stories about other people who felt like failures, or were treated harshly by peers, critics, family, and other disbelievers.

Collect a file of inspiring stories about mistakes that turned out well.

Follow your inspiration.

52
ACCENT THE POSITIVE

Always picture succeeding. Never let it fade. Always picture success no matter how badly things seem to be going in the moment.

~ Jessie Burton, author

Successful people always accent the positive—no matter how badly things may be going. Very often they use a wide array of different strategies to think and grow positively.

Whether you must overcome your ego or pride, or come to a practical realisation that giving in to forlorn thoughts will never be a winning formula, strive to model positivity.

When you let desire, not fear, propel you forward, magic happens. It's the Law of Attraction. The Law of Manifestation. The Law of Intention. But it only works if you stay positive. Negativity is a repellent. Positivity is a magnet, drawing abundance forward.

His Holiness The Dalai Lama once said, "Negative thoughts are like weeds—they grow untended, positive thoughts are like flowers—you need to nurture them every day."

Accenting the positive also means developing a warrior mindset and keeping any critics well away.

"Don't waste your time with explanations, people only hear what they want to hear," advises author Paulo Coelho. Listening too much to others, or overly seeking validation and approval, can hinder your success. Plenty of successful people have received scathing reviews, rejections and public humiliation from peers and critics, but they persevered anyway.

Few people know that *The Alchemist,* which has sold more than 65 million copies worldwide, was initially rejected. A small Brazilian company agreed to publish it but only 900 copies were printed and they declined to do a rerun. It wasn't until after Paulo Coelho's subsequent novel, *Brida,* was published that *The Alchemist* was revived and took off.

Failure is inevitable. Not everyone is going to love your writing. Many readers will take great pleasure in venting their dissatisfaction—whether they have downloaded your book for free, $0.99, $2.99, or more. Despite its huge popularity, even *The Alchemist* had 1-star reviews!

So, what to do? Sometimes I respond to negative feedback on Amazon, especially when I know it is undeserved. I figure many people will read my comments and then make their own assessment. Some authors welcome negative reviews, rationalising this makes the five-star reviews more credible.

As someone once said, "I can't give you the recipe for success, but I can failure—try to please everyone." Whatever approach you take, don't let rejection stop you. Accent the positive and figure out if there is anything you learn—even if this is just mastering the art of indifference.

No one ever truly knows what the market will do next, nor the music you hold inside! Seek growth and commit to continual improvement.

If you feel despondent and fear not being good enough, consider looking at the authors whose books you enjoy and read their "bad" reviews. Remind yourself that at some stage, almost everyone gets a bad rap.

Crack on with your next book!

Too many people die with regret. At least you will have the satisfaction of knowing you tried—and even better, that you kept going. Trust yourself and believe in your work!

Mining for Gold

How can you plant more positive thoughts and strengthen your optimism even when things look bleak?

How can you stay strong in the wake of criticism?

53

CHANGE YOUR BRAIN WITH MUSIC

I'm in an almost perpetual state of writer's block—writing is an occasional thing. What do I do about it? I drive around in my car and listen to music.

~ Aaron Sorkin, screenwriter

Boost your prosperous mindset by playing more music because it will stimulate you to new heights, help improve your mindset, and enable you to find creative answers and solutions to recurring challenges.

This may involve playing an instrument, perhaps by picking up one that you have studied in the past. It could also mean taking lessons.

Or it could just be a message for you to spend more time listening to music. Many people find it helpful to play music around their home and workplace continually.

"Music puts a spell on you," says author and intuitive coach Awen Finn. "Deep inside your favourite song lay the secret messages that unlock your psyche and all your potential."

Be sure to listen to uplifting tunes, as you are sensitive to the words and melodies. You may want to sing in order to express the music that's within you.

Along with the "Prosperity Playlist" I've compiled on Spotify, one of my favourite writing tools is focusatwill.com. I'm a big fan of this science-based tool. Not only do I love the music, but I love what it's doing for my productivity.

"The question many people want answered is how they can maximise focus so that their environment becomes less distracting and their attentional spotlight is continuously focused on their projects of the day," writes the team of researchers, scientists, and psychologists at Focus@Will.

"Auditory neuroscience and psychoacoustics (the psychology of sound perception) can help us answer this question," they say. "When you listen to music, sound waves hit your eardrums, are transferred to the cochlea in your inner ears, where microscopic cells called hair cells vibrate in response to the sound. The movement of the hair cells turns the mechanical energy of the sound wave into chemical signals that stimulate auditory nerves to fire action potentials."

Is this all too technical for you? Stay with us and learn how music can change the neurochemicals in your brain—and therefore, positively impact your mood and behaviour.

"Where does the signal go from there? The auditory pathway takes the encoded action potential signal from the ears to the brainstem cochlear nucleus and gets processed in a bunch of other brainstem locations. Finally, the signal moves to the thalamus and to the primary auditory cortex in the temporal lobe, which sits above your ears on each side of your head.

"When the signal gets into the brainstem, before it goes to the cortex and you become conscious of the sound, one of the areas that is likely to be activated is a bunch of neurons called the locus coeruleus. The locus coeruleus produces noradrenaline (also called norepinephrine), which is a stimulant for your brain.

"It sends noradrenaline to many other locations in your brain.

The areas targeted by the locus coeruleus are responsible for deciding how you are going to respond to a stimulus."

Author Joanna Penn says she finds great inspiration and creative power listening to playlists of rain and storms. What music feeds your creative juice and stimulates your prosperity mindset?

Mining for Gold

Create a soundtrack to feed your dreams. I still love Miley Cyrus's *The Climb*, particularly the encouraging lyrics to persist and persevere. "Ain't about how fast I get there. Ain't about what's waiting on the other side. It's the climb."

Consider working to a neuroscience-based soundtrack, or download an app like Focus@Will.

54

PATIENT PERSEVERANCE

The best thing I can tell you? It's one word. Persistence.

~ James Patterson, author

Knowing when to quit is one thing; knowing when to persevere another. Whether it's the weight of obstacles you face, the setbacks and the disappointments, the successes others seem to achieve more speedily, or the critical feedback from others who are impatient to see more evidence that you'll make it—never give up. Never, never, never give up.

Many prosperous authors' most enduring successes took years and years to achieve. Nora Roberts is probably the most successful romance novelist on the planet. Thirty-four of her titles are sold every minute and she earns an estimated $US60 million a year! But her success didn't happen in 6 months, a year, or even three.

She started writing back in the 1980's for Mills and Boon and then morphed into mainstream romance fiction—and other genres. So, I really shouldn't be discouraged when the three romance novels I published this year haven't filled my coffers with gold. Looking back, I also shouldn't have been discouraged by the feedback that I received early in my career that "my characters were dysfunctional." Instead of targeting Mills and Boon, the reviewer suggested that my romances seemed better suited to mainstream women's fiction—a path Roberts also pursued.

Along with Roberts' commitment to write characters she can personally identify with, it is her work ethic and her prolific output that really defines her. "Whatever I'm doing, I get very guilty if I don't put a good day's work in. I'm not one for making excuses. I had this Catholic upbringing. I was taught to finish what you start."

A prodigious work ethic, cultivated talent, commitment to finishing what she starts, over four different pen names, writing in a variety of genres, perseverance, and persistence are amongst the many things which have made her one of the world's most prosperous authors.

Award-winning, perennial bestselling author Jodi Picoult is the author of over twenty books, the last five of which debuted at No. 1 on the *New York Times* bestseller list. Her books have been translated into thirty-four languages, and four have been made into television movies, while another, *My Sister's Keeper*, was made into a film starring Cameron Diaz.

"I had over 100 rejection letters from agents. Finally, one woman who had never represented anyone in her life said she thought she could take me on. I jumped at the chance. She sold my first novel in three months," says Picoult.

Both authors, and others like them, wouldn't be where they are now if it weren't for their grit, persistence, and patient perseverance.

Mining for Gold

When you think of patience, perseverance, tenacity, and success, who comes to mind?

Who or what can help you to manifest more persistence? How can you keep your mind on your vision, your body moving towards your dreams, your heart warmed by the joy you will feel when you finally achieve success?

Identify three ways to strengthen your persistence by strengthening your willpower and self-discipline.

55

CULTIVATE HOPE

One's thoughts turn towards hope.

~ Leonardo da Vinci

Common obstacles to success include fear, self-doubt, and other crippling thoughts. But what if all you had to do to tame these "uglies" was to cultivate hope?

The power of hope is grounded firmly in spiritual and religious practices but also in science. Like the ancient Greeks and Romans, Leonardo da Vinci, and even 18th-century physicians, recognised the physiological effects of mind-power and hope on the body.

Successful medical outcomes, even when the intervention is a placebo, further evidence the impact of maintaining a positive expectation.

Dr. Joe Dispenza powerfully illustrates this fact in his fabulous book *You Are the Placebo: Making Your Mind Matter*.

If like me, and Joe Dispenza, you've manifested miracles in your own life by maintaining a positive expectation, you'll know the power of hope.

Thoughts *do* become things. Scientists Gregg Braden and Bruce Lipton, author of *The Biology of Belief,* have evidenced this.

But hope can only flourish when you believe that what you do can make a difference, that you recognise that you have choices and that your actions can create a future which differs from your present situation.

When you empower your belief in your ability to gain some control over your circumstances, you are no longer entirely at the mercy of forces outside yourself. You are back in the driving seat.

"Fearlessness is like a muscle. I know from my own life that the more I exercise it the more natural it becomes to not let my fears run me," says businesswoman, author, and founder of *The Huffington Post,* Arianna Huffington.

Would you rather be a failure at something you love than a failure at something you hate? It's a question worth considering.

What you believe has a tremendous influence on the likelihood of success. Reframe your fears and buoy your dreams with hope. Not "I'm afraid of failing," but "I hope to succeed," or something similar.

MINING FOR GOLD

How could you cultivate more hope? If you felt the fear and did it anyway, what's the best that could happen?

56

CHASE THE LIGHT

Having to fight hard has made me a better architect.

~ Dame Zaha Mohammad Hadid, architect

What's your default position when things go awry, obstacles challenge your resolve, technology goes belly-up, unforeseen demands on your time derail your plans, or you receive negative feedback?

Does your mood darken? Setbacks are normal foes you'll meet on the path to success, but how you greet them will determine the outcome.

Keep your thoughts light. You may need to bring out the big guns to wage war against doubt, despair, and other dark, heavy thoughts.

While they're often part of the journey to success, you will need to slay them to stay motivated and optimistic.

Prosperous people turn again and again toward the things that create light. They don't ignore the shadows, but they don't allow their mindset to be overloaded by darkness.

Acceptance, optimism, willpower, grit, stubborn determination, and a resolve to persevere are critical skills to cultivate, as is flexibility and the willingness to adapt.

Sometimes when it's all too hard and you need to hibernate, you may temporarily quit. You can take a lesson from nature in this regard.

But as sure as night follows day, and the seasons have their rhythm, if writing is your gift, your purpose, the thing that makes you happy, before long you'll be up and writing again.

Mining for Gold

Resist complaining and victim talk—it increases toxicity in your mind and body, hampering your progress.

Throw your energy into positivity—strive to engineer and implement solutions, no matter how small.

Ask for help if too much darkness creeps in.

Peer into the darkness and look for the gift. How can you move from darkness towards the light?

57

GOOD ENOUGH

Perfectionism will keep you poor.

~ Carla Coulson, photographer

"All of us failed to match our dream of perfection. So I rate us on the basis of our splendid failure to do the impossible," wrote author William Faulkner.

"In my opinion, if I could write all my work again, I am convinced that I would do it better, which is the healthiest condition for an artist. That's why he keeps on working, trying again; he believes each time that this time he will do it, bring it off.

"I believe that all artists are possessed by this silly ambition: they want to do something no one else has done before. They want to create something that's perfect. And they try, again and again, and they always fail. It seems to me that this is what truly motivates us.

"We keep on writing because nothing we write is good enough, or at least, as good as we think it should be. Or as good as we think it deserves to be," Faulkner says.

No story, no painting, no work of art is ever "finished." There's always something to change, to add, to remove. Good art pulsates with living energy—just like we do. There's always room for growth.

I know writers who have been "polishing" the same novel for tens of years. I was once one of them.

The challenge is knowing when to let go. Your task is to know when to stop editing and editing, reading and re-reading your work, over and over again.

The truth is if you overwork your creative project you can ruin its vibrancy, its essence, the energy that inspired you to create it in the first place. You run the risk of becoming paralysed by perfection, becoming sick of your creation, and losing your passion.

Someone once said, "It's like an itch you don't have to scratch, because every time you read your story, you'll always find something that needs to be changed. And if you feel like your story is perfect, just take a few weeks' break, then read it again. Suddenly, it won't feel as good as you previously thought."

Adopt a new mantra—the good enough mantra. Remind yourself "it's good enough." Know that, especially in this modern era of publishing, you can always go back to it later. But for now, you have to get things done, and you have to release them to the world.

Just like blowing bubbles, some will fly just for a few seconds, others will never get off the ground, while others will soar eternally towards the sky.

But working on the same writing project for much longer than is healthy is just as bad as starting a hundred different things and never finishing any of them.

I used to be afraid to let go of my work. I was terrified of what people might think of my books; I was worried they weren't good enough.

I still care, but I care less. I think it was Leonardo da Vinci who said that those who don't doubt their ability will never reach their heights.

An advance reader of this book said it was my best book yet. A reviewer of my previous book said the same thing. We all want to be better, but I know from experience that advancement is made only by moving forward.

If people like the books I write, great. If they don't, then I know that I have done the best I can do right now.

You only get better at writing by writing a lot, not by editing the same project for two decades.

Mining for Gold

Done is better than striving for the impossible—perfect. Avoid overworking your writing projects—let your work go out into the world knowing it is as good as it can be right now.

Set a definite date for completion.

Commit to continual improvement—in your new work and the books that follow.

FREE WORKBOOK!

The Passion Journal: The Effortless Path to Manifesting Your Love, Life, and Career Goals

Thank you for your interest in my new book.

To show my appreciation, I'm excited to be giving you another book for FREE!

Download the free *Passion Journal Workbook* here>>https://dl.bookfunnel.com/aepj97k2n1

I hope you enjoy it—it's dedicated to helping you live and work with passion, resilience and joy.

You'll also be subscribed to my newsletter and receive free giveaways, insights into my writing life, new release advance alerts and inspirational tips to help you live and work with passion, joy, and prosperity. Opt out at anytime.

CONCLUSION

"Know what you want and try to go beyond your own expectations. Improve your dancing, practice a lot, and set a very high goal, one that will be difficult to achieve. Because that is an artist's million: to go beyond one's limits. An artist who desires very little and achieves it has failed in life."

~ Paulo Coelho, in *The Spy*

There's never been a better time to harness the field of vast potential to make a living from your writing. But to grow your income, you need to grow, too.

"Your thoughts, feelings and beliefs are always engaging the fast field of pure potential," writes intuitive author Colette Baron-Reid.

Focus on your best life—regardless of any unfavourable or challenging outer conditions imposed on you by the physical world. You have stories to tell. You have divinely inspired talents to sow, nurture, harvest, and share with others.

Do the work, be a channel for inspiration, create big magic—thoughts really do become things and you will reap what you plant in your field of dreams.

Adopt a millionaire mindset—dream big, be audacious, take

inspired action, and fear less. Live more and experience the extraordinary life that awaits you. The power to create a life of prosperous significance lies within you.

Remember the truth about prosperity.

It's deeper than whether you have millions in the bank, three houses on the French Riviera, drive a limoncello coloured Lamborghini, or become a New York Times Bestseller.

Good fortune can mean counting the blessings for the seemingly simplest things—things that sadly too many of us take for granted. Your good fortune may include:

- Enjoying good health and mobility
- Being loved and loving in return
- Tapping into your infinite potential
- The ability to say, think, do, and write what you truly feel
- Living in a beautiful part of the world
- The ability to enchant and inspire others with your words
- Healing the world—one book at a time
- Money in the bank to cover the necessities of life
- Feeling happy with yourself
- Fulfilment
- Living authentically
- Being debt-free
- Making an extraordinary living from your writing

... Or something else.

What matters most is not how you define fortune, luck, prosperity, or whatever else you choose to name success. What matters is that the end result is meaningful to you.

If you continue to feel, think, and believe prosperously, then this unknown and unpredictable phenomenon will manifest in favourable outcomes—for you, those you love, and those drawn to you because of the beauty, power, and magic of your words.

if you infuse your life and work with your energy, power, talent and essence, who knows—100 years from today somebody may well be writing a book about you and the legacy you left.

You may think the outcome has to happen in a certain way, on a certain day, to reach your goal. But human willpower cannot make everything happen. Spirit has its own idea, of how the arrow flies, and upon what wind it travels.

It may not happen overnight, but if you follow your heart, maintain your focus, and take inspired action, your time will come.

I promise!

If by some strange twist of fate, it doesn't, at least you'll know you tried. A life of no regrets—now that's worth striving for.

Let the beauty you love and the words you yearn to write be the life that you live. Now go out and create great books!

To your prosperity, and with love,

P.S. In Book Two of the *Prosperity for Authors* series, Productivity Hacks: Do Less & Make More, you'll learn powerhouse productivity tools you can harness to help you finish what you start, create new books and take them to market so you can sell them faster.

We'll dive deeper into promotion strategies in Book Three of *The Prosperity for Authors* series, *Creating Soaring Profits*.

Sign up for my newsletter to be the first to know when new books in *The Prosperity for Authors* series are released, and receive practical tips to live prosperously here >>

Be the first to know when my guided meditations and self-hypnosis audios are released, and stay tuned for news of my *Prosperity for Authors* courses and webinars.

Sign up here http://eepurl.com/bEArfT

PLEASE LEAVE A REVIEW

Word of mouth is the most powerful marketing force in the universe. If you found this book useful, I'd appreciate you rating this book and leaving a review. You don't have to say much—just a few words about how the book helped you learn something new or made you feel.

"Your books are a fantastic resource and until now I never even thought to write a review. Going forward I will be reviewing more books. So many great ones out there and I want to support the amazing people that write them."
Great reviews help people find good books.

Thank you so much! I appreciate you!

PS: If you enjoyed this book, do me a small favour to help spread the word about it and share on Facebook, Twitter and other social networks.

ALSO BY THE AUTHOR

Transformational Super Kids:

The Little Princess
The Little Princess Can Fly
I Have to Grow
The Boy Who Cried

Mid-Life Career Rescue:

The Call for Change
What Makes You Happy
Employ Yourself
Job Search Strategies That Work
3 Book Box Set: The Call for Change, What Makes You Happy, Employ Yourself
4 Book Box Set: The Call for Change, What Makes You Happy, Employ Yourself, Job Search Strategies That Work

Master Life Coach:

Leonardo da Vinci: Life Coach
  Coco Chanel: Life Coach

The Art of Living:
How to Find Your Joy and Purpose
How to Find Your Passion and Purpose
How to Find Your Passion and Purpose Companion Workbook
Career Rescue: The Art and Science of Reinventing Your Career and Life
Boost Your Self-Esteem and Confidence
Anxiety Rescue
No! Why 'No' is the New 'Yes'
How to Find Your Joy and Purpose
How to Find Your Joy and Purpose Companion Workbook

The Art of Success:

Leonardo da Vinci
Coco Chanel

Journaling Prompts Series:

The Passion Journal
The Passion-Driven Business Planning Journal
How to Find Your Passion and Purpose 2 Book-Bundle Box Set

Health & Happiness:

The Happy, Healthy Artist
Stress Less. Love Life More
Bounce: Overcoming Adversity, Building Resilience and Finding Joy
Bounce Companion Workbook

Mindful Sobriety:

Mind Your Drink: The Surprising Joy of Sobriety

Also by the Author

Mind Over Mojitos: How Moderating Your Drinking Can Change Your Life:Easy Recipes for Happier Hours & a Joy-Filled Life
Your Beautiful Brain: Control Alcohol and Love Life More

Happy Sobriety:
Happy Sobriety: Non-Alcoholic Guilt-Free Drinks You'll Love
The Sobriety Journal
Happy Sobriety Two Book Bundle-Box Set: Alcohol and Guilt-Free Drinks You'll Love & *The Sobriety Journal*

Money Manifestation:

Financial Rescue: The Total Money Makeover: Create Wealth, Reduce Debt & Gain Freedom

The Prosperous Author:

Developing a Millionaire Mindset
Productivity Hacks: Do Less & Make More
Two Book Bundle-Box Set (Books 1-2)

Miracle Mindset:

Change Your Mindset: Millionaire Mindset Makeover: The Power of Purpose, Passion, & Perseverance

Non-Fiction:
  Where is Salvator Mundi?
  More of Cassandra's practical and inspiring workbooks on a range of career and life enhancing topics can be found on her website (www.cassandragaisford.com) and her author page at all good online bookstores.

ABOUT THE AUTHOR

CASSANDRA GAISFORD is best known as *The Queen of Uplifting Inspiration*.

A former holistic therapist, award-winning artist, and #1 best-selling author. A corporate escapee, she now lives and works from her idyllic lifestyle property overlooking the Bay of Islands in New Zealand.

Cassandra's unique blend of business experience and qualifications (BCA, Dip Psych.), creative skills, and wellness and holistic training (Dip Counselling, Reiki Master Teacher) blends pragmatism and commercial savvy with rare and unique insight and out-of-the-box-thinking for anyone wanting to achieve an extraordinary life.

Writing as Mollie Mathews (www.molliemathews.com), she is also known by her fans for her "sensual, beautiful, empowered stories enveloped in true romance." Her love stories have resonated with a global audience. She has been featured in magazines, television, and radio. A graduate of Victoria University, she has given keynote speeches at romance writers conventions and international seminars.

Mollie passionately believes in the power of romance to transform people's lives. Her stories are unashamedly positive, optimistic, full of fun and sizzling passion.

Both Cassandra and Mollie love all the arts, traveling, orchids, and all things inspiring, uplifting, and beautiful.

FURTHER RESOURCES

Surf The Net

www.whatthebleep.com—a powerful and inspiring site emphasizing quantum physics and the transformational power of thought.

www.heartmath.org—comprehensive information and tools help you access your intuitive insight and heart-based knowledge. Validated and supported by science-based research. Check out the additional information about your heart-brain.

Join polymath Tim Ferris and learn from his interesting and informative guests on The Tim Ferris Show http://fourhourworkweek.com/podcast/.

Listen to podcasts which inspire you to become the best version of your writing self—*Joanna Penn's podcast* is very helpful for "authorpreneurs" http://www.thecreativepenn.com/podcasts. I also love Neil Patel's podcast for savvy marketing strategies http://neilpatel.com/podcast.

Experience the transformative power of hypnosis. One of my favourite hypnosis sites is the UK-based Uncommon Knowledge. On their website http://www.hypnosisdownloads.com you'll find a range of self-hypnosis mp3 audios, including The Millionaire Mindset program.

Celebrity hypnotherapist and author Marissa Peer is another favourite source of subconscious reprogramming and liberation —www.marisapeer.com.

What beliefs are holding you back? Check out Peer's Youtube clip "How To Teach Your Mind That Everything Is Available To You" here —https://www.youtube.com/watch?v=IKeaAbM2kJg

Enjoy James Clear's fabulous blog content and receive further self-improvement tips based on proven scientific research: http://jamesclear.com/articles

Tim Ferriss recommends a couple of apps for those wanting some help getting started with meditation—Headspace (www.headspace.com) or Calm (www.calm.com).

Books

Master your millionaire mindset with T. Harv Eker's book, *Secrets of the Millionaire Mind: Mastering the Inner Game of Wealth.*

Find your ONE thing with Gary Keller in *The One Thing: The Surprisingly Simple Truth Behind Extraordinary Results.*

Learn from masters in a diverse cross-section of fields—pick up a copy of Tim Ferriss' *Tool of Titans.*

Celebrate being an outlier and learn why clocking up 10,000 hours will help you succeed in Malcolm Gladwell's *Outliers: The Story of Success.*

Struggling in an extroverted world? Introverts are enjoying a renaissance, fuelled in part by Susan Cain's terrific bestseller, *Quiet: The Power of Introverts in a World That Can't Stop Talking.*

Copy-cat your way to success with Austin Kleon's great book, *Steal Like An Artist.*

Roll up your sleeves and bring out the big guns to win your creative battle with *The War of Art* by Steven Pressfield.

Power up with a new personality—read Breaking the Habit of Being Yourself: How to Lose Your Mind and Create a New One by Dr. Joe Dispenza.
Unleash the power of your mind by reading *You Are the Placebo: Making Your Mind Matter,* by Dr. Joe Dispenza.

Manifest your prosperity with Rhonda Byrne in her popular book, *The Secret.*

Ensure you don't starve by reading Jeff Goins collated wisdom in *Real Artists Don't Starve: Timeless Strategies for Thriving in the New Creative Age.*
Fortify your faith with Julia Cameron's book, *Faith and Will.*
Learn how to live an inspired life with Tarot cards and other oracles. Read Jessa Crispin's book, *The Creative Tarot: A Modern Guide to an Inspired Life.*
As intuitive counsellor, psychic medium and author Collette-Baron-Reid writes in one of her books, "As a recovered addict and alcoholic, 29 years clean and sober at the time of this writing, I have devoted myself to changing my old story about being a victim, powerless, angry and hard done by, too different, too much, and not enough."
Check out all of Collette's books, including: *Uncharted: The Journey Through Uncertainty to Infinite Possibility* and *Messages from Spirit: The Extraordinary Power of Oracles, Omens, and Signs.*

STAY IN TOUCH

Become a fan and Continue To Be Supported, Encouraged, and Inspired

Subscribe to my newsletter and follow me on BookBub (https://www.bookbub.com/profile/cassandra-gaisford) and be the first to know about my new releases and giveaways

www.cassandragaisford.com
www.facebook.com/powerfulcreativity
www.instagram.com/cassandragaisford
www.youtube.com/cassandragaisfordnz
www.pinterest.com/CassandraNZ
www.linkedin.com/in/cassandragaisford
www.twitter.com/CassandraNZ

And please, do check out some of my videos where I share strategies and tips to stress less and love life more—http://www.youtube.com/cassandragaisfordnz

I invite you to share your stories and experiences in our Prosperous Author Community. We'd love to hear from you! To join, visit https://www.facebook.com/TheProsperousAuthor

BLOG

Subscribe and be inspired by regular posts to help you increase your wellness, follow your bliss, slay self-doubt, and sustain healthy habits.

Learn more about how to achieve happiness and success at work and life by visiting my blog:

www.cassandragaisford.com/archives

SPEAKING EVENTS

Cassandra is available internationally for speaking events aimed at wellness strategies, motivation, inspiration and as a keynote speaker.

She has an enthusiastic, humorous and passionate style of delivery and is celebrated for her ability to motivate, inspire and enlighten.

For information navigate to www.cassandragaisford.com/contact/speaking

To ask Cassandra to come and speak at your workplace or conference, contact: cassandra@cassandragaisford.com

NEWSLETTERS

For inspiring tools and helpful tips subscribe to Cassandra's free newsletters here:
http://www.cassandragaisford.com

Sign up now and receive a free eBook to help you find your passion and purpose!
http://eepurl.com/bEArfT

ACKNOWLEDGMENTS

Thank you to all the prosperous authors and creative people who've made a living from their creativity for inspiring me.

Thank you to all the advance readers. Your willingness to help, cheerleading, and constructive feedback definitely made this book more successful.

A huge thank you also to my amazing Prosperous Author buddies Cate Walker and Amy Stokes for your beautiful and thorough editing.

Thank you, too, for purchasing and reading this book. I hope you enjoyed it and that you'll be encouraged to follow your path with heart and create an extraordinary living from your writing.

And to the love of my life—Lorenzo, my Templar Knight. Thank you for believing in me—and reminding me that the life of a starving artist holds no potential.

Thank you, dear reader, for trusting me to guide you. I really hope you loved this book as much as I truly enjoyed writing it. And I hope it aids your success, as I have succeeded and flourished during the many hours I spent writing and applying the principles I share in this book.

Here's to an extraordinary level of happiness and success in all lives.

Copyright © 2017, 2019 Cassandra Gaisford

Published by Blue Giraffe Publishing 2019

Blue Giraffe Publishing is a division of Worklife Solutions Ltd.

Cover Design by Cassandra Gaisford

All rights reserved. No part of this publication may be reproduced, distributed, or transmitted in any form or by any means, including photocopying, recording, or other electronic or mechanical methods, without the prior written permission of the author or publisher, except in the case of brief quotations embodied in reviews and certain other non-commercial uses permitted by copyright law.

Neither the publisher nor the author are engaged in rendering professional advice or services to the individual reader. The ideas, procedures, and suggestions contained in this book are not intended as a substitute for psychotherapy, counselling, or consulting with your physician.

The intent of the author is only to offer information of a general nature to help you in your quest for emotional, physical, and spiritual well-being.

Any use of information in this book is at the reader's discretion and risk. Neither the author nor the publisher can be held responsible for any loss, claim or damage arising out of the use, or misuse, of the suggestions made, the failure to take medical advice or for any material on third party websites.

ISBN PRINT: 978-0-9941484-0-7

ISBN EBOOK: 978-0-9951288-7-3

ISBN HARDCOVER: 978-0-9951288-8-0

Third Edition

❦ Created with Vellum

www.ingramcontent.com/pod-product-compliance
Lightning Source LLC
Chambersburg PA
CBHW030436010526
44118CB00011B/654